THE
JOY OF KNITTING
COMPANION

THE

JOY OF KNITTING

COMPANION

Lisa R. Myers

RUNNING PRESS
PHILADELPHIA · LONDON

9 8 7 6 5 4 3 2 1

Digit on the right indicates the number of this printing

Library of Congress Control Number 2002108259

ISBN 0-7624-1451-0

Cover photography by Michael Weiss

Interior illustrations by Dorothy Reinhardt

Technical illustrations by Alicia Freile

Jacket design by Alicia Freile

Interior design by e Bond

Edited by Jennifer Worick

Typography: Sabon and Trade Gothic

This book may be ordered by mail from the publisher.

Please include $2.50 for postage and handling.

But try your bookstore first!

Running Press Book Publishers

125 South Twenty-second Street

Philadelphia, Pennsylvania 19103-4399

Visit us on the web!

www.runningpress.com

For my daughters,
Diana and Eva,
in the hope that they too will
find fulfilling work when they grow up

Contents

Knitting in the New World

Knitting seems to be everywhere these days. Television and movie stars say in interviews that they knit on the set between takes. *The Wall Street Journal* ran an article on the difficulty of knitting on airplanes in our newly security-conscious world. Maybe fans of *Sex and the City* should have seen it as an omen when, in an episode from the 2002 season, a character announced that she was knitting baby booties. The times, they are a-changin'.

The Joy of Knitting was published a few days before September 11, 2001. While I hope its view of knitting reflected some of the virtues we've begun to re-examine since then, I would like to make my views more explicit here. Knitting exemplifies, is an outlet for, or can help you cultivate any or all of the following: patience,

generosity, industry, empathy, compassion, charity, and good humor. Some of these sound very old-fashioned; in fact, the very idea of virtue might have seemed hopelessly out of date until recently. But we live in a new world, and we are discovering that we have no more outgrown our ancestors' ways of thinking about good behavior than we have the tribal resentments and furies of centuries ago. Technology changes, but human nature seemingly does not.

As I write this, barely a year after the terrorist attacks, news coverage marking the anniversary is torn between two contradictory claims: everything has changed, and any change means the terrorists have won. On the one hand, commentators and person-on-the-street interviews examine the ways in which our lives have changed (airport security, a new appreciation for loved ones and everyday joys). On the other hand, there's a strong impulse to appear unchanged, to demonstrate that "they" can't break "our" spirit or seriously challenge the American way of life. From the moment the stock market reopened and the Administration urged Americans to continue spending in order to keep the economy strong, it has seemed as if the freedom we're willing to go to war to defend may be merely the freedom to go to the mall.

I'd like to propose an alternative. The poet Marianne Moore wrote that "There never was a war that was / not inward." ("In Distrust of Merits," *Nevertheless,* 1944.) Let's not pretend that we're unchanged. We live like most of the rest of the world now: with the threat of sudden violence, aware of hatreds that simmer in our midst and on the other side of the globe. Without descending into blind self-absorption, let's investigate and renew some of those old virtues: duty, charity, simplicity.

In other words, let's knit.

• • •

The Joy of Knitting was a reading book. This companion is more hands-on, more how-to. There are chapters on planning projects, instructions for accessories and information on how to customize them, and general information about yarn that should help you when shopping on your own. Much of the information in each of the "Basics" chapters could be applied to one or more of the others, however. Instructions for making fringe are in Chapter 6 (see page 90), but you might want to put fringe on a bag (see Chapter 7); instructions for stranded or fair-isle knitting are in Chapter 5 (see page 79), but you might want to use a band of fair-isle patterning around the bottom of a hat (see Chapter 3). Various techniques are included throughout the book.

Chapter 1

Selecting a Project

Is beginning a project your favorite part, or is finishing one? What about the planning and daydreaming before you begin? There's a place at the end of this book to record sketches and ideas for future projects; this chapter, however, will help you get focused when you're really getting ready to begin.

Lots of people come into my shop and pronounce, "I want to make a sweater." Then they stand and look at me as if I'm going to say, "Okay, here's one," and hand them a bag of yarn and needles.

I'm not.

They've done some preliminary work—they know they're not making a hat, and they probably know who's going to wear the sweater—but they're just getting started.

Review the box on page 14 for a list of suggested questions to help you begin thinking about a sweater. These questions are meant to trigger others that are more individual, like the age-old debate between "How many purple sweaters can one person have?" and "I like purple. I wear a lot of purple. If everything I have goes with purple, what could be more useful than another purple sweater?" You don't have to answer all the questions in advance, of course. You'll have an easier time finding a pattern if you're open to, say, the various possibilities of a sexy, lightweight, closefitting cardigan than if you know it has to be a sexy, lightweight, closefitting cardigan with a broad, shallow V-neck.

So, armed with some preliminary information, you go to your local yarn shop and say, "I want to make myself a bulky pullover to wear outside in the Fall." Maybe the shop will have something perfect hanging on display, and all you'll have to do is say, "Does this yarn come in brown?" More likely, you'll have to browse through some yarn possibilities, or some pattern possibilities, or both.

Most people start by looking at patterns, but some begin with yarn. If you know what weight or texture you want for the garment, yarn can be a great place to start. Say for the moment you are looking for bulky—whether because you've got a new puppy and really need that walking-in-the-woods sweater, or because you want something quick to knit on big needles. Whoever's helping you at the shop can direct you to the bulky yarns. Now you start looking and touching, considering any swatches that are available, imagining what each yarn will do well. Is it kind of scratchy, with a somewhat stiff swatch? Think jacket. Is it remarkably soft and light? Just because it's "meant" for scarves doesn't mean you can't make a sweater. If it's hairy and multi-colored, think simple (i.e., no pattern stitches).

If a yarn appeals to you, but you aren't getting any clear ideas about its "destiny," ask. Maybe there's a sample hat on display that you've overlooked, or maybe there are patterns for it in books or magazines. You don't have to use a pattern written for that yarn, of course, but looking at one or more will give you more information about how bulky it is to wear, or how busy the tweed is.

If you like the yarn, ask where to find some patterns that would work for the kind of garment you want. This part of the search isn't an exact science, so give the shop assistant some leeway. There will be patterns that definitely would work, and some that might or might not—until the swatching and measuring start, no one knows for sure. If you love the yarn, you can ask to see patterns, or you can go right to the next step: "I'm definitely going to use this yarn in this color, so can I take a skein and make a swatch to narrow down the pattern possibilities?" (You may want to take one intermediate step: "I love this yarn. About how many will I need for a pullover for myself? Okay, I can afford that.")

Your stockinette swatch will tell you what gauge you like for the yarn, which will tell you roughly which patterns are eligible. There may still be designs that interest you that require more swatching (Does the cable show clearly enough? Does this yarn get too "drapey" in that stitch pattern?). Two yarns may have the same stockinette gauge but behave differently in other stitch textures, so that they aren't completely interchangeable.

If you haven't narrowed your ideas down very far, or if cut is the most important thing to you, looking at yarn can be overwhelming and confusing. If you'd rather work in the other direction, grab some pattern books and make yourself comfortable. Though as knitters we tend to think in terms of gauge or function—bulky, outerwear, pullover—magazine editors clearly think in other terms, like "blue" or "beach." Someone at the shop may be able to show you one book or leaflet with a few bulky sweaters all in one place, but you'll probably have to comb through a lot more patterns of every kind all jumbled together. At my shop, we have separate binders for women, men, and children, and for Spring/Summer and Fall/Winter, but that's as far as we can go. Half the pullover patterns have cardigans on the same page, and plenty of leaflets have adults and children together (maybe with a dog too). If we put each pattern every place it belonged, we would need twice as much space for binders, and when something sold out in one place we'd be looking for it in three others before we knew whether to reorder. Even so, there would still be all the bound books and magazines, which obviously can't be sorted by individual patterns.

In other words, you're probably going to have to see a lot of sweaters that have little or nothing to do with what you want before you find the perfect thing. Sometimes, something else will reach out and grab your attention and completely derail you—suddenly you're captivated by the kind of dressy sweater you were searching for last season—which isn't necessarily a terrible thing.

There's a knack to choosing a pattern from a photo. It's a little like catalog shopping: you have to get past the unconscious belief that, if you knit that sweater, you'll look like the model . . . or have that house, or steal away for country weekends in the Fall. We are all pretty sophisticated consumers of advertising by now, and we know how television commercials attempt to seduce us. But a surprising amount of the healthy suspicion with which we view ads evaporates when we're confronted with a Rowan magazine. What exactly do you plan to do with a super-bulky sleeveless wool sweater with a huge cowl neck? And why are you shocked that it's not a slenderizing fit? A word to the wise: with few exceptions, the models in sweater patterns or magazines are as skinny as professional models anywhere else.

So my advice is to look at the sweater, and not the person in it, as much as possible. Look at its bulk, its drape, and as many of its design features as you can see: length, neck width and/or depth, tightness of cuff and sleeve, shoulder seam placement. Some magazines like *Vogue Knitting* and *Interweave Knits* will give you hints in the caption or the head note to the pattern: "This close-fitting turtleneck comes just to the hipbone," for instance. There's plenty you can change about the pattern, but only if you know that you want to!

Assuming you're not committed to choosing

Some useful questions when planning a project

- Do you want to make something for yourself or for someone else?
- Something to wear or something to use? The former includes sweaters, hats, gloves, mittens, scarves, socks, slippers, legwarmers, shawls, ponchos, dresses, skirts, bikinis, etc. The latter includes bags, placemats, tea cozies, stuffed animals, golf club covers, pillows, afghans, etc.
- If it's a sweater: Pullover or cardigan? Indoor wear or outdoor? Bulky or fine? Warm or lightweight? For Fall/Winter or Spring/Summer? Classic, retro, or up-to-the-minute styling? Pockets? Close-fitting, boxy, or oversized? Length? Neckline: Round, square, scoop, V-neck, asymmetrical, boat? If round neck, crew, mock turtle, turtle, roll, or cowl? Sleeveless, cap-sleeve, short sleeve, three-quarter, or long? If it's a cardigan: Button, zip, toggles, frogs, or no closure?
- Multicolored yarn or solid?
- One yarn for the whole project, or different ones combined? (The latter includes intarsia, fair-isle, striped, blocked, entrelac, appliqué or other embellishment, and even two different yarns stranded together.)
- Plain stockinette, knit/purl pattern stitch, lace, cables?
- Color?
- Should the fabric be soft and loose, snug and stretchy, dense, stiff?
- Must the yarn be machine washable? Dryable?
- Does the wearer/user have any known fiber allergies?
- What are the price constraints?

only patterns produced by the yarn manufacturers, if you've got a particular yarn in mind, you're going to guess at which sweaters are appropriate, and then check the instructions to see if the gauge matches. Sometimes the shopkeeper can give you hints—"Your swatch is 4 stitches to the inch, so keep an eye out for any pattern that calls for Manos, Montera, or All-Seasons Cotton." Most of the time, however, it's just a slow process of checking and checking again until you find a match. Be patient, and don't blame the person at the shop for not showing you the perfect pattern immediately. Most people say, "Just a really simple cardigan with a round neck," but they don't mean it, as we find out (and they should realize as well) when the first three patterns we pull out are rejected. They're looking for something more specific than they can articulate, so they're just going to have to keep looking until they see something that strikes them.

I'll tell you a little secret: we've got some terrific simple patterns that aren't photographed very glamorously—mannequins, not live models; blank white backgrounds, not elaborate sets with props—and most knitters reject them out of hand. It's a failure of imagination. If we have a sample knit up in the shop, people jump on it, saying, "That's so cute!" or "It's perfect!" But if we don't, we can't persuade them that it is, in fact, exactly what they want. Nothing doing.

Sometimes the leap of imagination required is significant, I admit. "Picture it on a less dorky-looking guy" is a tall order. "Like this one, only without the fringe and sequins" leaves you wondering what would be left. It's hard to know how the sexy angora number will translate into a Shetland wool tweed, even if the gauge is the same—it's certainly not going to cling as much (which is a good thing considering how scratchy the tweed can be), but will that cowl drape at all, or will it look like a strange, oversized turtleneck? Experience will improve your ability to make these judgments. In the meantime, that's what yarn shop employees (and other knitters) are for.

A popular question from both non-knitters and new knitters is, "How long will it take to knit this sweater?" There's no answer to that question—every knitter's experience will be different. I might be able to guess how long a particular sweater would take *me*, but that's not what the person asking wants to know. Most knitters want to know how long it would take *them* (though some want to know how long it would take their mother/wife/boyfriend to knit it for them). And even if I could say, "This sweater might take me forty hours, so a beginner might need sixty," it wouldn't help much. Like a kid on a car trip asking "Are we there yet?", most people are asking, "When will it be done?"

For that, I can help you make some guesses. The key questions are "How much time can you give the project?" and "How badly do you want it?" If the dishes are done and the kids are in bed by 8:00 every night, and you are going to sit in front of the television knitting until 11:00 five nights a week, you're going to see some serious progress. If you work several eight-hour shifts a week as a phone-sex operator and your boss doesn't care if you knit while you work, a sweater every three weeks may be a perfectly reasonable expectation. If you commute by train from New Haven to Manhattan and aren't prone to motion sickness, the sky's the limit.

If, on the other hand, you work full-time and are going to school three nights a week, progress will be slower. If you're training for a marathon while taking care of three kids under the age of 5, your days are pretty well packed. If you've got yoga classes two nights a week, season tickets to the orchestra and the ballet, and a very active book group, you'd best avoid projects with deadlines.

Some sweaters do take longer than others. The knitter who can whip out 2 inches per hour of plain stockinette just can't burn through a cabled sweater at the same pace—you lose a couple seconds twisting the cables, no matter what you do.

But that's not the whole story: if that speedy knitter finds stockinette boring, or dislikes the yarn, or is feeling ambivalent about the girlfriend to whom she promised the sweater, she's going to find excuses not to pick the project up at all. She will get the cable sweater done faster because she enjoys it more, or because she's more enthusiastic about it.

What else speeds a project up? Loving the yarn; snow days, or a Cary Grant fim festival on cable; having an idea for a new project that's just around the corner if you can finish this one up; the return of cool weather in the Fall; promising yourself that you have to do two rows—just two rows—on it every day, but then you can put it down if you want and work on another project. What else slows a project down? Having to rip out stitches because you made a mistake; worrying that you are going to run out of yarn;

suspecting that it won't fit when it's finished. Some of these are things you can plan for next time, some not.

If you need to refresh yourself on a stalled project, consider throwing a UFO (Un-Finished Object) party. Invite fellow knitters to bring one or more of their UFOs, and then everyone agrees to work on nothing else during the afternoon or evening. You can help each other solve problems that may have caused the halt in the first place, and you'll see some real progress from the intensive focus. Often this kind of jump-start is all you need to get a UFO back on track.

Reading a chart

Charted knitting patterns are increasing in popularity, and with good reason: they're easier to proofread, and therefore more accurate (very little is more frustrating than ripping and reknitting several times, only to find out that the error is in the printed instructions). They take less space and are therefore more cost-effective to print. They're easier for knitters to modify (from flat knitting to knitting in the round, for instance). And, with a little practice, they're easier to read and follow than the old row-by-row verbal instructions. Here's what you need to know:

First, think of the chart as trying to look like a piece of knitting. Each square represents one stitch, and the symbol in the square tells the knitter how to work that stitch. In order to make your knitting look like the chart, you start at the bottom of the chart and work each row of squares as one row of stitches. Since the first stitch of your row is the one at the right-hand end, the first square you consult on the chart is the one at the right-hand end (assuming you're beginning with a right-side row). The chart will often have a little "1" at this end

of the row, to show you that the first row, and in fact all odd-numbered rows, starts here.

Somewhere near the chart, or in the information and abbreviations area of the pattern, will be a glossary of the various symbols used (see chart on page 19). The symbol in the square shows what the stitch should look like on the right side of the fabric—that is, the outside of the garment, the public side. How you work the stitch will depend on whether you're working from the right side or the wrong side. For instance, a blank square usually means a knit stitch; but if I'm on an even-numbered or wrong-side row, I'll have to purl that stitch to make it come up like a knit on the other side. This is why the glossary defines so many symbols twice, as in "Purl on right side, Knit on wrong side."

Sometimes the chart will show as many squares as there are stitches on your needles, and you'll just work across the whole row stitch by stitch. More often, the chart will show only some of the stitches. For a cable, for example, down the middle of a sweater, the chart might show just the 12 stitches in the center of the row, and the instructions will tell you to follow the chart over the center 12 stitches while keeping the rest of the stitches in reverse stockinette stitch. The easiest way to do this is to place a marker on your needle just before and just after these 12 stitches. Then you know that all the stitches outside the markers are purled on the right side and knit on the wrong side, and when you get to the marker, you look at the chart.

If the whole piece uses the same stitch pattern, the chart will usually show only one repeat—that is, one complete pattern. For instance, for moss stitch, the chart would look like this:

If your row were 32 stitches wide, you'd knit the first 2 stitches, then purl the next 2 stitches, then go back to the beginning of the chart row and repeat those 4 stitches as many times as necessary (i.e. 7) to complete the row.

Sometimes a pattern begins and ends a little differently at the edges of the fabric. A chart will show this by giving a few stitches outside the marked repeat. If the chart looks like this:

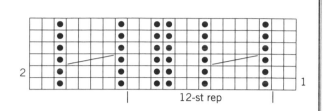

you would begin Row 1 by knitting 2 stitches, then repeat the p1-k4-p1-k2-p2-k2 sequence as many times as necessary until there were 8 stitches left in the row, then work the last 8 stitches as shown (p1-k4-p1-k2). (For more on pattern multiples and repeats, see page 20.)

If you are knitting back and forth, you would turn the work around at the end of the row and prepare to work back across Row 2. But now the first stitch on your needle is the stitch you just worked—the *last* stitch of Row 1, the stitch at the *left* side of the chart. So for Row 2, you read the chart from left to right, working the 8 stitches as shown outside the repeat bracket (remember, this is a wrong-side row, so those 8 stitches are now p2, k1, p4, k1) and then repeating the set of 12 stitches until there are only 2 stitches left.

If you're knitting back and forth in rows, the chart is read in this zigzag way. But what if you were knitting in the round? You'd never turn the work around, so every row would be a right-side row. When you went to begin

Round 2, the first stitch would be directly above the first stitch of Round 1, so you'd read the chart again from the right-hand end; and because you're still looking at the outside of the fabric, the first stitches would be two knits again. This is one of the ways charts are more versatile than verbal directions: if you knit a scarf and liked the pattern, you can now repeat the same pattern on, say, a matching hat without having to translate all the instructions for the even-numbered rows. Just look at the chart and follow the instructions to make your stitch look like the one in the "picture."

Charts invite you to think about the knitting in a visual way—not "cable to the front next or cable to the back?" but "Okay, now two cables leaning in towards each other."

Common Chart Symbols

☐	k on RS, p on WS
⊡	p on RS, k on WS
◹	k2tog on RS, p2tog on WS
◺	ssk on RS, p2tog through back of loop on WS
△	slip 2 sts tog knitwise, k1, pass 2 slipped sts over
b	k through back of loop on RS, p through back of loop on WS
B	make bobble—will be defined elsewhere in pattern
O	yarn over
◿	k 2nd st on left ndl, then k 1st st, then slip both sts off needle
◺	reach *behind* 1st st on left ndl to knit 2nd st, then k 1st st, then slip both off ndl
◿◻	C2B: slip next 2sts to cable ndl and hold at back of work, k2, then k2 from cable ndl
◺◻	C2F: slip next 2 sts to cable ndl and hold at front of work, k2, then k2 from cable ndl
⊡⊡◿	slip next 2 sts to cable ndl and hold at back of work, k2, then p2 from cable ndl
◺⊡⊡	slip next 2 sts to cable ndl and hold at front of work, p2, then k2 from cable ndl

Pattern multiples and repeats

As you read through this or any other book with stitch patterns, you may encounter phrases like "Multiples of 4" or "Multiple of 6 sts plus 2." This information indicates how many stitches you'll need to make the instructions "work." For instance, a rib pattern of 2 knit stitches followed by 2 purl stitches might be described as a 4-stitch repeat—k2, p2 is one pattern unit, and you'd repeat those 4 stitches across the row. As long as your row contains a multiple of 4 stitches, all you have to do is k2, p2; the wrong-side row comes out right if you just repeat k2, p2 too.

But now suppose you're doing that same rib as the bottom edge of a sweater. The designer may decide that the edge will look nicer if it is symmetrical—that is, if the row begins and ends the same way, rather than beginning with 2 knits and ending with 2 purls. So she'll add 2 extra knit stitches at the end to match the 2 at the beginning. But this changes the way the instructions have to be written: the knitter will repeat "k2, p2" across the row, but then there will be 2 stitches left over that have to be knitted. One way to write this is: "Row 1: (K2, p2) across, end k2." But the wrong-side row changes too: when you turn around to go back, you have to begin by purling the first 2 stitches. One way to write this would be, "Row 2: (P2, k2) across, end p2." Another would be:
"Row 2: Work sts as they appear," that is, if a stitch looks like a purl, purl it, and if it looks like a knit, knit it.

Thus when a stitch pattern says, "Multiple of x sts," it means that the number of stitches in your row needs to be evenly divisible by x for the pattern to work. And when it says, "Multiple of x sts plus y," it means that some number of sts have been added into the instructions to balance the pattern out. To test and see if a particular number of stitches works for the pattern as given, you'd first subtract y and then divide what's left by x—if it comes out even, you're fine.

Two favorite stitches

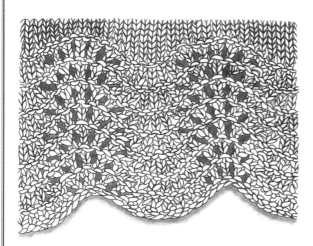

St. John's Wort, or Mock Cable

This tiny stitch looks a lot like a cable but isn't. It's popular in lacy items and baby things, though it would also be lovely on a hat or mitten or at the edge of a flared cuff.

New Shale

Also known as Feather and Fan, this is a traditional pattern that makes a wavy or scalloped edge.

Multiple of 11 sts.
Rows 1 and 3 (RS): K.
Row 2: K.
Row 4: *P2tog twice, (yo, p1) 3x, yo, p2tog twice, rep from * to end of row.
Repeat Rows 1–4.

Multiple of 4 sts plus 1.
Rows 1 and 5 (WS): K1, *p3, k1; rep from * to end of row.
Row 2: P1, *slip 1, k2, pass slipped st over 2 k sts and off the end of the needle, p1; rep from * to end of row.
Row 3: K1, *p1, yo, p1, k1; rep from * to end of row.
Rows 4 and 6: P1, *k3, p1; rep from * to end of row.
Repeat Rows 1–6.

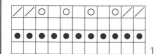

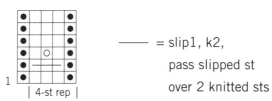

—— = slip1, k2, pass slipped st over 2 knitted sts

Chapter 2

Yarn Notes

Chapter 1 talked about whole projects and project beginnings. Now it's time to pause and take a closer look at yarn. This section works in two ways: first, you will get the outline to construct your own "field guide" to major types of yarn, recording your own impressions and experiences with various fibers and structures. Second, you will have space to begin a personalized "database," capturing more detailed information about specific brand names. You can fill in an entry or two for each project you knit, but from time to time you may also want to play with a yarn just to play. As a break from a big project, or between projects, or when you're traveling and can't carry along your current work, it can be fun to take a skein of something new and different and just see what it can do.

Here's how I might "test-drive" a yarn:

First, look at the label: what size needles does the manufacturer recommend to achieve what gauge? I usually start with the suggested needle size. Can't find the needle size on the label? Look for a tiny picture of two crossed needles, maybe with a crochet hook below them. There should be one or more numbers to either side and/or above or below. If there's only one set of numbers—say, "4–5"—it is usually for European needle sizes, which are measured in millimeters. You'll find a conversion chart on the front flap of this book. Otherwise, you'll likely see "4–5" on one side and "US #6–#8" on the other.

Then I cast on a few more than the number of stitches that is "supposed to" yield 4 inches (10 cm). Can't find the stitch gauge on the label?

Look for a tiny picture that might represent a square of knitting. There should be one number underneath and another number at the side. The number at the bottom—maybe followed by the letter M—is the number of stitches in 4 inches. (The first letter of the word for "stitches" is m in both French, *mailles,* and German, *Maschen.)* The number to the side is the number of rows in 4 inches, and may be followed by the letter R (for *rang* and *Reihe.)*

I knit two rows for a bottom edge, then switch to the following pattern for a stockinette-stitch swatch with garter edging: Row 1: Knit. Row 2: K2, purl to last 2 sts, k2. I repeat these 2 rows until the piece is just about square, then knit 2 rows and bind off.

Well, actually, that's not quite what I do. When the swatch is maybe an inch or an inch and a half wide, I stop and consider how it looks and feels. If it seems way too tight or way too loose, I rip it out and start again with a different size needle. If I just want to try out the yarn, I don't concern myself with measuring the gauge at this stage. I just want to see how the yarn responds and at what needle size and gauge it seems most comfortable.

Once I have a stockinette fabric that I like, I'll measure. I might make a note like "Looks nice at 4½ sts = 1". Hard to believe the label thinks it belongs at 3½." This is one of the pleasures of swatching for its own sake: I have

Double knitting

One of the questions I hear most often in my shop is, "What does DK mean?" Marked on a yarn label or pattern, "DK" stands for "double knitting." It's a designation of a yarn weight, something between what Americans mean by sport and worsted. It originated in England in the period of shortage that followed World War II: "double knitting" yarn was spun to a thickness that could be used for patterns calling for either gauge. Nowadays, a DK-weight yarn is basically anything that can be knit comfortably at 5½ stitches to the inch.

no anxiety about "getting the gauge" because I'm not trying to make the yarn work for any particular pattern. This is all about what works best for the yarn itself.

At this point, I might stop and bind off the swatch. Or, if I'm making a swatch for the shop or just feeling curious, I'll make another swatch—this one at the label's gauge—to show people. I may even wash the second swatch, just to see if it "fluffs up" and looks more "right" at that gauge (some yarns do).

I'm also influenced by hunches about possible uses for the yarn. If I am considering using it for socks, I'll knit a very tight swatch using a smaller needle (again, guessing at how many stitches will give me 4 inches and casting on about that number). If I think the yarn will felt well, I'll definitely make an extra-loose swatch to be fulled later. And I'll consider treating some or all of these stockinette swatches—not just fulling the loose swatch, but machine-washing the basic swatch if the label says I can, for instance. If I make a dense swatch for socks, I'll do an abrasion test. I tie the swatch around my wrist inside my shirt cuff and wear it every day for a week, then look for signs of pilling.

Next, I'll try some stitch patterns. I almost always do seed stitch, because I like it and so do most other people, and it's a fair example of all of the small simple texture stitches. I usually do a swatch with some sort of cable—either three simple 2-across-2 twists separated by an inch or so of reverse stockinette, or any cable combination that has caught my eye lately (yes, sometimes these swatches get wider than 4 inches). Especially with cotton yarns, I try one or more lace patterns—maybe a very simple one with an eyelet here and there, then something more all-over and open. If the pattern repeat means I need a few stitches more or less than my 4 inches, that's fine. For lace, I tend to round the numbers downward, since the pattern will probably show better if it's knit a little loosely or blocked to spread it open. I try not to judge the allover lace patterns until I have enough to stretch out wide. Put another way, I try to remember as I swatch that almost all lace patterns look like nothing at all until they're vigorously blocked.

Through all this, I'm making notes—even while I'm knitting each swatch—because I'll have forgotten much of what I'm thinking by the time all the swatches are completed and dressed. ("Dressed" is the technical term for all those finishing treatments.) Ultimately, I expect to assemble the swatches into a baby blanket or scrap afghan; that's why I try to keep them about the same size. But if a swatch isn't working—if it just looks lousy, or the pattern doesn't show, or whatever—I rip it out rather than wasting the yarn. But I do make notes about the failures before I rip, so that I haven't wasted my time, either. ("Too fluffy for lace patterns—fills up all the holes." "Even a large cable hardly showed, because the colors are so active.")

CALCULATION AND CONVERSION TIPS

There are two questions that pose enormous interest to knitters—How much yarn will this take? And, how much yarn do I have? The first question comes into play from the moment you start your first project, but the second one doesn't arise until sometime later. When the only yarn you have is still unopened in its original wrapper, you know how much yarn you have: whatever it

Fabric care symbols

 Washable. This mostly means that the yarn is not afraid of water, although washing machines may still provide too much agitation and stretch the garment.

 Hand washable. Any temperature indication is centigrade; the most common ones are 30 for cold water and 40 for warm.

 Do not wash by hand or machine.

 Machine washable.

 Machine dryable.

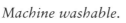 *Do not tumble dry.*

   Ironing. The dots on the side (one, two, or three) indicate a cool, warm, or hot iron.

 Do not iron.

 Household bleach. The letters "CL" indicate chlorine bleach permitted.

 Do not bleach.

 Dry clean. With the letter "F," dry clean using fluorocarbon- or petroleum-based solvents; with "P," those above plus perchlorethylene-based solvents; with "A," dry cleanable with all solvents.

 Do not dry clean.

says on the label. The trouble starts when you have yarn left after finishing a project. Sooner or later you're going to wonder, *Is there enough left for a matching hat?*, *Could I make stripes in my next scarf?*, and so forth.

As I've explained elsewhere, the amount of yarn a project requires is a matter of yardage. So when you ask how much yarn you have, you want the answer to be in yards (or meters, if that's what you prefer). You could unroll the ball and measure it, but there are easier ways. You'll need to establish two key pieces of information: weight and grist. "Grist" is related to the word "grind," and it has to do with how thickly or thinly a yarn has been spun—thin yarn has more yards per pound (ypp) then thick yarn does. Grist allows you to convert weight of yarn to length.

Weight: If it's a large skein or several, use a deli scale. The person behind the counter may look at you a little funny, but if you ask nicely, you can usually put your yarn (preferably in a lightweight plastic bag) on the scale for a moment. The number you get will be in hundredths of a pound, but we can work with that.

For smaller amounts, try a kitchen or postage scale. The old-fashioned postage scale is the only thing I know that works well for amounts under a couple of ounces (with the exception of a lab balance, which is terrific if you have access to one). If you've never used a postage scale, it works like this: a wire pointer is suspended from the middle of a flat piece of metal that has a hook at the top and a clip at one side. When you put a piece of mail in the clip and suspend the scale by the hook, the pointer indicates the letter's weight along markings at the bottom edge. But the clip can also be used to suspend a ball of yarn with the same results. This is a great contraption: inexpensive, easy to store, virtually unbreakable (if the wire parts get lost or broken, you can replace them with unbent paperclips).

So, step 1, establish the weight of your yarn. Step 2, find out the *grist*. This is easy if you know the yarn's name: ideally, you still have the label, which tells you the weight and yardage of the original skein. If you don't have the label but know the name, call your local yarn shop or look on the internet—anyone selling the yarn can tell you how many yards per skein or ounce or kilo, and most shops have a copy of a yarn-substitution guide called "Valuable Knitting Information" that includes lots of discontinued yarns as well.

Now, the tough case: you have no idea what this yarn is, or what it's made of. It's time for another piece of specialized equipment, the McMorran balance. This is fundamentally a balance with a fixed weight. One end of the balance arm has a notch in which you lay a strand of yarn, and then you snip tiny pieces off the strand until the balance rests perfectly level in its little groove. Then you measure the length of the strand as carefully as you can and multiply the result (in inches) by 100. This number is the approximate number of yards in a pound of that yarn.

Your shop may have a McMorran balance; shops that specialize in spinning and/or weaving supplies are more likely to. You may decide that this problem is going to come up repeatedly, so consider investing about thirty dollars to own one yourself. Look on the internet to order one by mail.

Now you know weight and grist. Get out your calculator and use these tables to solve for yardage:

Conversion Factors
1 lb = 16 oz. = 457.12 grams
1 meter = 39.37 inches = 1.0936 yards
50 grams = 1.75 oz.

Equations
Length = grist x weight
Yards = (yards per pound) x
(weight in pounds)

The most common, and most complicated, case: you know how much yarn you have in hundredths of a pound (from the deli scale) and how many meters were in a 50-gram ball:

Yards = (meters in 50g ball) x (1.0936 yards per meter) ÷ (9.1424 50g balls in 1 lb) x (weight from the scale, in hundredths of a lb)

9.1424: How many 50g balls are in 1 pound? 457.12 grams in a pound, divided by 50 grams in each ball, = 9.1424.

How much yarn will this take?

Here's a chart showing approximately how far a yard of yarn goes at various gauges. The first column is gauge; the second, how many square inches of knitted fabric one yard of yarn will make; the third, how many yards of yarn are required to make one square inch of fabric. All calculations are for stockinette stitch.

Gauge	Sq. in/yd	# Yards/ Sq. in of fabric
3	2.13	.47
3.5	2.04	.49
4	1.72	.58
4.5	1.6	.63
5	1.46	.68
5.5	1.29	.78
6	.98	1.02

How to read a yarn label

There's more information on the typical yarn label than you'd ever imagine. Some things are absolutely required if the yarn is to be sold in any European Economic Union member country—the yarn's name, the manufacturer's name, the weight and/or length of the skein, the fiber content, the country of origin. Beyond that, you can expect washing instructions, gauge information, a guess at needle size, and even some idea of how many skeins a typical project might require. Here's what to look for:

Yarn name: Usually the biggest letters on the label. Pay attention; someday, you'll want to talk to someone about this yarn.

Manufacturer's name: More precisely, brand name. The yarn was manufactured by a mill, but the mill may have sold it to the company that put the name and label on it. Some companies—like Rowan—have their own mills and do most or all of their own spinning. Others—like Trendsetter—shop around at huge trade shows in Europe to find interesting yarns, and then contract with the mills that produce them. Note that the brand name on the label may not be your "source" of the yarn, either; the shop where you buy yarn probably orders most European brands through their U.S. distributors. To wit, yarns by Lang are imported to the U.S. by Berroco, which also manufactures yarn of its own; yarns by Mission Falls or Colinette are imported to the U.S. by Unique Kolours, which is solely a distributor and doesn't make any yarn under its own label.

Fiber content: "Wool" is *laine* in French, *wolle* in German. "Cotton" is *coton* in French, *baumwolle* ("tree-wool"—don't you love it?) in German. Alpaca, angora, and mohair are recognizably similar words in all three languages. "Silk" is *soie* or *seide*. Rayon may be called "viscose." All the synthetics are basically the same words in all European languages.

Color number: Look for a number that may appear stamped rather than printed. "Color" may be abbreviated "col," or "sh" for "shade." Don't despair if the label is not in English; *couleur* in French or *Farbe* in several Germanic languages mean the same thing. Really small producers like hand-dyers may stamp (or even hand-write) a color's name on the label instead of a number—"Patina," "Arabian Nights," "Songbird," and "Elizabeth Cady Stanton" are, I kid you not, yarn colors.

Dye lot: Usually found beneath or next to the color number. *Partie* is the equivalent in both French and German. Make sure all the skeins for a project have the same dye lot number.

Weight: Usually measured in grams, abbreviated "g.," or ounces, abbreviated "oz." If the label is in Greek, Russian, or Japanese, look for a number that ends in zero. To convert back and forth between grams and ounces, see page 28.

Length: This is maybe the most useful one of all for most knitters. It may be given in yards ("yds."), but more likely in meters ("m."). To convert back and forth between yards and meters, see page 28.

Gauge: Big American manufacturers like Classic Elite, Berroco, and Reynolds give English-language gauge statements like "5¼ stitches = 1 inch." European manufacturers have gone over to a sign system that takes up less space and is multilingual. Look for a small square that looks either like a grid or like a bit of stockinette fabric. There will be numbers above, below, and to either side of it. The number at the bottom is the stitch gauge (it may be followed by the letter M for *mailles* in French or *Maschen* in German). This is always the number of stitches in 10 cm, or 4 inches, of stockinette stitch. The number along the side is the row gauge (possibly followed by the letter R for *rangs* or *Reihen*). This is the number of rows in 10 cm of stockinette. Most yarns behave well when knit a little tighter or a little looser

than the stated gauge, but the gauge on the label provides a convenient estimate.

Needle size: Somewhere near the gauge information you may find a clear English phrase ("Needles: US #8") or a little picture of two crossed knitting needles, possibly with a crochet hook beside or underneath them. *Unless the needle size specifically says "US," assume that the numbers are in millimeters,* the European needle sizing system. To convert back and forth between U.S. and European needle sizes, see the needle gauge on the front flap of this book.

Yarn requirements: If you are lucky enough to find a tiny picture of the outline of a sweater, the manufacturer is giving you a hint about how many skeins will make a garment. Below or beside the picture will be a number like "Gr. 40," which indicates the size (German *Grosse*) in question (here, 40 cm circumference at underarm). If the picture has short sleeves, the calculations assume a short-sleeved garment. Nearby will be another number, usually divisible by 50, which is the weight of yarn required, in grams. So if the number is 450 and the skein you're holding is 50 grams, the picture is trying to tell you that a woman's medium short-sleeved pullover will take about 9 skeins.

Your yarn database

Here's a head-start on assembling your own database of yarns.

Yarn Name: Manos del Uruguay

Manufacturer: Manos del Uruguay

Fiber content: 100% wool

Weight of skein or ball: 100 g.

Yardage: 138 yards

Recommended needle size: US #9

Recommended gauge: 4 sts = 1"

General description of yarn: Slightly thick-and-thin single ply, with a fair amount of light-dark variation in the color as well (it's hand-spun and hand-dyed). Some colors are nearly solid, some more varied. Also comes in space-dyed versions that combine at least three colors (though it often looks like many more).

Notes on swatch characteristics and the "knitting experience": Feels great in the hands as you are knitting. At 4 sts = 1", a good basic heavy weight for hats and sweaters. Small stitch texture patterns show off the yarn's natural variations, and cables read very well, but detailed knit-purl patterns get lost. Pretty soft, but probably too warm for most indoor pullovers. Fair-isle patterns likewise would get very bulky and warm, but intarsia and other multicolor designs are great; the colors are wonderful together, and there are lots of them. **Potential uses:** Hats, cardigans, bulky ski-type sweaters or jackets. Knit on a slightly larger needle, good for scarves. Great for "decorator" afghans or throws; won't stand up to machine washing, so not for real workhorse blankets. Likewise probably not durable enough for socks. Felts beautifully, though—slippers, hats, bags?

Additional Notes:

_____

_____

_____

_____

Yarn Name: La Gran

Manufacturer: Classic Elite

Fiber content: 76.5% mohair, 17.5% wool, 6% nylon

Weight of skein or ball: 50 g.

Yardage: 90 yards

Recommended needle size: US #9

Recommended gauge: 4 sts = 1"

General description of yarn: A classic "brushed" mohair: wisps of fiber seem to hover over the fabric like a haze. The wool and nylon are mostly at the core, holding the yarn together; all you notice is the mohair. Lots of luster, silky feel, takes dye well like most mohairs but also comes in pale, soft, and/or muted colors.

Notes on swatch characteristics and the "knitting experience": The swatch looks and feels very light but is very warm. Uses a bigger needle than you might think when looking at the skinny core; all that hair needs breathing room. Easy to knit with but tough to rip out: the fibers seem to grow together as time passes. Ribs show okay and cables are good, but forget complicated patterns. On the other hand, lace is terrific—light and airy, and openwork would keep the garment from being too warm. Needs a big needle to show clearly, though, and/or serious blocking.

Potential uses: Sweaters, scarves, shawls, fuzzy hats and mittens. Adds warmth without weight to ponchos, capes, throws, afghans. Despite its ethereal look, mohair is strong and durable—if it comes back from the cleaner (or off the drying rack) looking flat, brush it lightly until the fibers fluff up again.

Additional Notes:

_____

_____

_____

_____

_____

_____

_____

Yarn Name: Lite Lopi

Manufacturer: Reynolds

Fiber content: 100% wool

Weight of skein or ball: 50 g.

Yardage: 109 yards

Recommended needle size: US #8

Recommended gauge: $4\frac{1}{2}$ sts = 1"

General description of yarn: Minimally-spun Icelandic-style singles. Some natural heathering, as if the undyed fiber varied in shade. Fairly coarse wool. Very wide color range available, including an excellent selection of undyed grays and browns.

Notes on swatch characteristics and the "knitting experience": Swatch shows patterns very well—just about all kinds of patterns, from knit-purl textures to fair-isle to lace and cables. Conveniently lighter in weight than traditional Lopi, but still coarse and somewhat itchy. Not very strong; very tight knitters may find that it breaks as they work (try a smaller needle size than usual, as well as a lighter hand).

Potential uses: Good for outerwear, ski sweaters, bags, and any felting project.

Additional Notes:

_____

_____

_____

_____

_____

_____

_____

_____

_____

_____

_____

Yarn Name: Cotton Classic

Manufacturer: Tahki

Fiber content: 100% cotton

Weight of skein or ball: 50 g.

Yardage: 108 yards

Recommended needle size: US #6

Recommended gauge: 5 sts = 1"

General description of yarn: Cabled, mercerized cotton. Many, many colors, especially bright ones. Repeated washings will eventually dull the high shine, but the yarn is very slow to pill or fray.

Notes on swatch characteristics and the "knitting experience": Cotton's lack of "give" or "bounce" makes it a little less forgiving than wool—the knitter has to provide all the tension, which can be tiresome, and uneven stitches will show more in the final fabric. That said, Cotton Classic is among the best of them: beautiful colors, durable, a little more elasticity and softness than most.

Potential uses: Spring and summer sweaters and tops; baby and kid stuff; bags.

Additional Notes:

_____

_____

_____

_____

_____

_____

_____

_____

_____

_____

_____

_____

_____

Yarn Name: Snuggly DK
Manufacturer: Sirdar
Fiber content: 55% nylon, 45% acrylic

Weight of skein or ball: 50 g.
Yardage: 193 yards
Recommended needle size: US #6
Recommended gauge: 5½ sts = 1"

General description of yarn: A basic, plied yarn; very soft; not at all itchy. Available in a standard range of bright colors, plus two series of pastels (one simply light, one incredibly pale), very few darks (navy, black, maroon), and no subtle or "off" shades. Machine wash and tumble dry; wears like iron; won't pill like some of the first- and second-generation acrylics did.

Notes on swatch characteristics and the "knitting experience": Has a nice bouncy feel, like a wool yarn; excellent memory. Good stitch definition for cables and knit-purl patterns; for lace, only simple openwork is very effective, as the synthetic fiber won't hold the strong blocking necessary for crisp "read" on complex patterns.

Potential uses: Designed and marketed as a baby yarn, for which it is excellent. Thousands of patterns are out there—and it is interchangeable with Peter Pan DK and several other common baby yarns (same yardage, too). Availability of bright colors makes it useful for toddlers and older children as well. A reasonable option for socks if you must avoid wool, though most of the colors are a little strong.

Additional Notes:

Yarn Name:_____Manufacturer: _____

Fiber content: _____

Weight of skein or ball:_____Yardage: _____

Recommended needle size: _____Recommended gauge: _____

General description of yarn: _____

_____

Notes on swatch characteristics and the "knitting experience":

_____

_____

_____

_____

Potential uses: _____

_____

Yarn Name:_____Manufacturer: _____

Fiber content: _____

Weight of skein or ball:_____Yardage: _____

Recommended needle size: _____Recommended gauge: _____

General description of yarn: _____

_____

Notes on swatch characteristics and the "knitting experience":

_____

_____

_____

_____

Potential uses: _____

_____

Yarn Name:_____Manufacturer: _____

Fiber content: _____

Weight of skein or ball:_____Yardage: _____

Recommended needle size: _____Recommended gauge: _____

General description of yarn: _____

_____

Notes on swatch characteristics and the "knitting experience":

_____

_____

_____

_____

Potential uses: _____

_____

Yarn Name:_____Manufacturer: _____

Fiber content: _____

Weight of skein or ball:_____Yardage: _____

Recommended needle size: _____Recommended gauge: _____

General description of yarn: _____

_____

Notes on swatch characteristics and the "knitting experience":

_____

_____

_____

_____

Potential uses: _____

_____

Yarn Name:_____**Manufacturer:** _____

Fiber content: _____

Weight of skein or ball:_____**Yardage:** _____

Recommended needle size: _____**Recommended gauge:** _____

General description of yarn: _____

_____

Notes on swatch characteristics and the "knitting experience":

_____

_____

_____

_____

Potential uses: _____

_____

Yarn Name:_____**Manufacturer:** _____

Fiber content: _____

Weight of skein or ball:_____**Yardage:** _____

Recommended needle size: _____**Recommended gauge:** _____

General description of yarn: _____

Notes on swatch characteristics and the "knitting experience":

_____

_____

_____

_____

Potential uses: _____

_____

Yarn Name:_____Manufacturer: _____

Fiber content: _____

Weight of skein or ball:_____Yardage: _____

Recommended needle size: _____Recommended gauge: _____

General description of yarn: _____

_____

Notes on swatch characteristics and the "knitting experience":

_____

_____

_____

_____

Potential uses: _____

_____

Yarn Name:_____Manufacturer: _____

Fiber content: _____

Weight of skein or ball:_____Yardage: _____

Recommended needle size: _____Recommended gauge: _____

General description of yarn: _____

_____

Notes on swatch characteristics and the "knitting experience":

_____

_____

_____

_____

Potential uses: _____

_____

Yarn Name:_____Manufacturer: _____

Fiber content: _____

Weight of skein or ball:_____Yardage: _____

Recommended needle size: _____Recommended gauge: _____

General description of yarn: _____

_____

Notes on swatch characteristics and the "knitting experience":

_____

_____

_____

_____

Potential uses: _____

_____

Yarn Name:_____Manufacturer: _____

Fiber content: _____

Weight of skein or ball:_____Yardage: _____

Recommended needle size: _____Recommended gauge: _____

General description of yarn: _____

_____

Notes on swatch characteristics and the "knitting experience":

_____

_____

_____

_____

Potential uses: _____

_____

Yarn Name:_____Manufacturer: _____

Fiber content: _____

Weight of skein or ball:_____Yardage: _____

Recommended needle size: _____Recommended gauge: _____

General description of yarn: _____

_____

Notes on swatch characteristics and the "knitting experience":

_____

_____

_____

_____

Potential uses: _____

_____

Yarn Name:_____Manufacturer: _____

Fiber content: _____

Weight of skein or ball:_____Yardage: _____

Recommended needle size: _____Recommended gauge: _____

General description of yarn: _____

_____

Notes on swatch characteristics and the "knitting experience":

_____

_____

_____

_____

Potential uses: _____

_____

Yarn Name:_____Manufacturer: _____

Fiber content: _____

Weight of skein or ball:_____Yardage: _____

Recommended needle size: _____Recommended gauge: _____

General description of yarn: _____

_____

Notes on swatch characteristics and the "knitting experience":

_____

_____

_____

_____

Potential uses: _____

_____

Yarn Name:_____Manufacturer: _____

Fiber content: _____

Weight of skein or ball:_____Yardage: _____

Recommended needle size: _____Recommended gauge: _____

General description of yarn: _____

_____

Notes on swatch characteristics and the "knitting experience":

_____

_____

_____

_____

Potential uses: _____

_____

Yarn Name:_____Manufacturer: _____

Fiber content: _____

Weight of skein or ball:_____Yardage: _____

Recommended needle size: _____Recommended gauge: _____

General description of yarn: _____

_____

Notes on swatch characteristics and the "knitting experience":

_____

_____

_____

_____

Potential uses: _____

_____

Yarn Name:_____Manufacturer: _____

Fiber content: _____

Weight of skein or ball:_____Yardage: _____

Recommended needle size: _____Recommended gauge: _____

General description of yarn: _____

_____

Notes on swatch characteristics and the "knitting experience":

_____

_____

_____

_____

Potential uses: _____

_____

Yarn Name:_____Manufacturer: _____

Fiber content: _____

Weight of skein or ball:_____Yardage: _____

Recommended needle size: _____Recommended gauge: _____

General description of yarn: _____

_____

Notes on swatch characteristics and the "knitting experience":

_____

_____

_____

_____

Potential uses: _____

_____

Yarn Name:_____Manufacturer: _____

Fiber content: _____

Weight of skein or ball:_____Yardage: _____

Recommended needle size: _____Recommended gauge: _____

General description of yarn: _____

_____

Notes on swatch characteristics and the "knitting experience":

_____

_____

_____

_____

Potential uses: _____

_____

Chapter 3

The Basics: Hats

Everybody needs a hat. Don't give me any of this nonsense about hats mussing your hair or not being manly. It's cold out there. All the cool skiers (or snowboarders, for the younger set) wear hats. If they're sized properly, they needn't disturb your hair. The winter landscape needs a little more interest, what with cities full of gray buildings, gray slush, and all of you in your gray, black, or navy coats. Let's perk it up, people!

There are beautiful, complicated hats out there to be knitted (see Anna Zilboorg's *45 Fine and Fanciful Hats* and Nicky Epstein's *The Knit Hat Book* for stellar examples), but there are plenty of ridiculously quick and simple, incredibly useful ones, too. And no, there's no reason why you shouldn't make up your own pattern.

First, a little hat anatomy. Most hats are knitted starting at the bottom and ending at the top. At the bottom, they either have a brim or they don't. If they don't they may have a fold-up cuff or a band. Above that is the crown, the deep straight area where it is easy to place a pattern. Then at the top there's the closure area, the part where you usually decrease into the center, and then there either is or isn't a pompom.

So, from the bottom: you could make the usual ribbed cuff or band. Even in this age of miracle fibers and technological wonders, lots of store-bought hats are made of knit fabrics with ribbed cuffs. Why? Because this is stuff knitting does brilliantly. A hat should be warm and fit snugly. Ribbing is just the ticket. If you're short of time or yarn, 2 to 3 inches of ribbing will hold a hat in place. But if you knit twice that depth, you can fold it up for double the warmth over

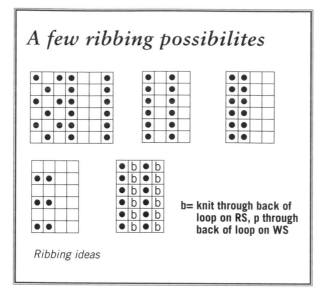

A few ribbing possibilites

b= knit through back of loop on RS, p through back of loop on WS

Ribbing ideas

the ears. You can do a k1,p1 rib, or a k2,p2, or something uneven like k3,p2, or exotic combinations with seed or garter stitch in between. There are also twisted or cable combinations, which grip even more snugly.

If you don't want a ribbed band, you can try garter stitch. This is kind of tricky, though, because you have to be fairly precise about size and gauge. Ribbing will expand and contract to suit the wearer's head size, but garter stitch won't (much). And if you tend to cast on tightly, the bottom edge of the band may be uncomfortable. On the other hand, some yarns tend to stretch out over time, so the band that starts out right may loosen later. One solution is to find fine-gauge elastic and knit it in with the yarn for the band. (Or wait until later and weave the elastic in along the inside.)

If you just cast on and start knitting, you'll have a hat with a rolled edge, which is both easy and cute. This is the one you want if you're worried about your hair, and you'll want to choose a yarn that's light and lofty. This is about as close as you can get to a knitted brim; knitted fabric, no matter how tightly worked, really doesn't have the rigidity for a real brim (not to mention the trouble you'd have getting it to hold a particular angle).

Next comes the crown. Basic hats and caps work straight up, giving you an open area for almost any type of pattern. You could continue any rib you started at the cuff. Or try a big fair isle snowflake pattern, or a series of smaller borders. (You *are* knitting this in the round, aren't you? For pity's sake, knit your hats in the round!) This is a great moment for horizontal stripes—two colors in 1-inch bands, or random widths of three or more colors, or 2 rows each of 8 colors repeated again and again. Try a few simple cables, or one big ornate Celtic knot.

If you want a beret or tam, of course, you won't keep knitting straight up from the band. Instead, you'll increase—either all at once as soon as the band ends, or gradually over 2 to 3 inches of stockinette. In either case, it's usually not more than 4 inches from the top edge of the band until the decreasing starts to shape the top.

Now, the top shaping is where the options really diversify. In theory, the task is simple: you

Yarn guidelines for hats

- Warmth.
- Itchiness.
- Elasticity/Memory.
- Water resistance. Bear in mind that wool continues to insulate even when it is wet.
- Compactibility. The hat that is scrunched into a pocket gets lost less easily than the hat that is tucked into a sleeve.
- Color.

need to reduce the number of stitches from whatever it is at the crown circumference to almost nothing at the center. Depending on yarn gauge and so forth, a hat usually ends with somewhere between 6 and 20 stitches being pulled tight and fastened off. Here are two extremes: first, the paper bag top, in which you bind off all the stitches, then gather them together like a kid holding a lunch bag and tie yarn tightly around a spot an inch or two below the top. Second, the stocking cap, in which you decrease a few stitches at a time *v-e-r-y s-l-o-w-l-y* so that you have knit 2 feet of hat before you reach the final point. Most hats, of course, fall somewhere in between. Tams, for instance, decrease at a rate related to pi, so that they wind up flat like pancakes. It's all a matter of how fast you decrease; how much height are you

adding in the time it takes to work those decreases? See page 48-49 for specifics on numbers and ratios, and page 54 for specifics on various decreases.

HOW TO MAKE A HAT

1. Measure your gauge, both stitch and row, over whatever stitch or pattern you plan to use for the body.

2. If possible, measure the wearer's head around the widest point the hat will cover, usually the upper part of the ears and right above the eyebrows. If it is not possible to measure, assume the following:

Small full-term newborn:	14–15"
Large newborn–6 months:	16"
1–4 years:	17"
6–10 years:	18"
Kids' Large:	19"
Kids' XL/Adult XS:	20"
Adult Small:	21"
Adult Medium:	22"
Adult Large:	23"

Consider that men's heads, while actually larger than women's, may sometimes seem smaller because women typically have more hair.

3. Multiply gauge by size, then adjust. Does your pattern need a specific multiple? Are you

planning a rib or other band pattern that requires a particular multiple? Do you know what top shaping you are going to do, and does it require a particular multiple? When in doubt, round down, so the hat does not fall into the eyes.

4. Cast on. If your band is going to be rolled or ribbed, use the number you arrived at in step 3. If it is garter stitch, reduce that number by about 5 percent. Use a 16-inch circular needle (yes, even for the baby sizes) either in whatever size got you the gauge in step 1 or in something a size or two smaller if you like a tight band.

5. Join into a round, being careful not to twist, and work band or cuff. Berets have from 1 to 2½ inches of band. The cuff on a man's watch cap can be 2–3 inches deep. The cuff on a baby's hat might be 1 inch deep. If you're working a roll, you don't have to do anything: the fabric will roll up by itself as you knit, but then eventually it will stop and you'll start to see straight fabric hanging between the needle and the roll. There's no calculating how much roll you will get; it seems to vary by knitter more than by yarn.

6. Change to crown pattern, increasing if you cast on a reduced number for the band or cuff, increasing or decreasing if you need a different pattern multiple than the band used, increasing a lot for a beret or tam, and changing needle size if you had started with a smaller one.

7. How deep should the crown be? This depends, inconveniently, on the top shaping—on how much deeper the whole hat will get once the shaping starts. After you've been knitting the crown for a while, you need to plan the end of the hat and work backwards from there. So . . .

8. Plan the top shaping. See pages 52 and 53 for instruction on different types of decreases.

Option 1: Square. Two corners and a straight seam in between, often with pompoms at the points. The top of the hat should be above the top of the head: figure 6 inches for a baby, 8 inches for child, and as much as 10 inches for an adult (you're going to lose some height when the bottom is spread open on a head). Either bind off all the stitches and sew the seam flat, or divide the stitches in half onto two needles and do a three-needle bind-off.

Option 2: Flat tam. Do your geometry homework: the circumference of your circle is, say, 25 inches (because you increased above the band to make a big flat disc), and 125 stitches. You need to reduce this number to about 5 or 10 stitches in exactly the time it takes to get from perimeter to center. A straight line from the outside edge to the center is the radius of the circle. What's the radius of a 25-inch circle? Remember $c = 2\pi r$? That is, the circumference is two times pi times the radius. Pi, or π, you may recall, is about 3.14159. So 25 inches is 2 times 3.14159 times the radius, or 25 inches = 6.28318r. 25÷6.28318 = 3.97888, or *very* close to 4 inches.

Stay with me. It's 4 inches from the edge of the circle to the center. How many rows will you have to knit to fill those 4 inches? Go back to your gauge: say you were getting 7 rows to the inch. So it'll take 28 rows to get to the center; you have 28 rows in which to decrease 125 stitches to 5.

For aesthetics as well as convenience, let's assume you decrease the same number of stitches every time—for this example, let's say 5. If you want to decrease from 125 down to 5 or 10, that's 115 or 120 stitches to get rid of; at 5 stitches per decrease round, you'll need 23 or 24 decrease rounds. To spread those evenly throughout 28 rounds of knitting, you'd decrease almost every round—maybe decrease on 5 consecutive rounds, then skip the sixth. You may prefer to decrease every other round 4 or 5 times right away, and then do the rest of the decreases consecutively.

The easiest thing to do is to imagine the circle divided into 5 even wedges, each 25 stitches wide, then knit 2 together at the end of each wedge. So the first decrease round is (k23, k2tog) repeated 5 times. For the second decrease round, though, each wedge has shrunk to 24 stitches, so it is (k22, k2tog) 5 times. This method makes a kind of swirling star pattern at the top of the hat.

Suppose, however, that you want a more traditional-looking tam, without the swirl. For that, you need a centered double decrease, so

you'll be losing 10 stitches each round. This means you'll only need 12 decrease rounds out of 28, or a little less than every other. In fact, there will have to be about four moments when you skip 2 rounds between decreases. So the first rounds might go like this: decrease, plain, decrease, plain, decrease, plain, plain.

You'll also have to move the decrease points in the round, though, because they won't be centered decreases if one of them is at the end of the round. Now each pie wedge should go like this: k11, double decrease, k11. On the second decrease round, each wedge will be 2 stitches smaller, so it will be k10, double decrease, k10.

The tam top is the most complicated case, but it sets up all the easier ones. If you want something that conforms more closely to the contours of the head (i.e., a cap of some sort), you'll decrease more quickly, that is, without working the full number of rows needed to reach the center. This might mean more decreases per round—say, 8 instead of 5—or it might mean hurrying up at the end: 5 or 6 decreases every round until 20 or 30 stitches remain, then a round of k2tog all around to reduce that by half, then cut the yarn and fasten off. ("Fasten off," in this context, means pull the cut end of the yarn through the remaining stitches, draw tight, and secure the end well.)

You may wonder, "Why not decrease *really* quickly—say, k2tog all the way around twice in

---

Yarn requirements

- At a gauge of 2½ stitches = 1", 87 yards of yarn will make an adult's rolled-edge hat.
- At a gauge of 3½ stitches = 1", 83 yards of yarn will make an adult's rolled-edge hat.
- At 4 stitches = 1", 135 yards will make an adult's ribbed watch cap with cuff.
- At 5 stitches = 1", 160 yards will make an adult's big floppy beret.

---

a row?" You can. Try it; you may like it. But very swift decreasing will gather the fabric together, until it ripples or bunches in the center—not an effect everyone appreciates. Also, done this way, some of the crown depth you've already worked will suddenly be pulled toward the center to cover the top of the head, so the hat that seemed long enough when you began to decrease no longer reaches the top of your ears.

A moment's consideration of stocking caps: They are easy. Figure 4 or 5 decreases per round, then space those rounds an inch apart. If you started with an adult's medium at 4½ stitches per inch—maybe 94 stitches—that will be 22 decrease rounds of 4 stitches per round, and 22 inches of hat above the wearer's head (or, more precisely, trailing down behind the wearer's head). How do you spread 4 decreases evenly through a 94-stitch round? You don't. When you're ready to begin decreasing, you first decrease 2 stitches randomly throughout the round, then begin the "real" decreases on the next round with nice convenient 23-stitch quarters.

What happens to your crown pattern during the top shaping? Best of luck. This is the real reason so many watch caps are ribbed at the cuff but stockinette thereafter—the decreases would disrupt the rib, and it seems to look better than changing to stockinette just at the very top. This is also the reason plenty of watch caps have sudden last-minute bunchy decreases: to minimize the area of disrupted rib. (If your gauge and size allow you to use a multiple of 8 stitches, you can find instructions for a watch cap with the decreases integrated into the rib in *The Joy of Knitting,* page 87.)

If you plan ahead, you may be able to continue at least some of your cables in between the decreases, at least for a while. Fair-isle patterns are best abandoned, though, unless you've got specific charts for a tam. Most knit-purl patterns are pretty hopeless (a possible exception: seed stitch can be made to work if you do centered double decreases—what used to be p1, k1, p1 becomes just p1, since there's a knit before and after it). The usual thing to do in all these cases is abandon the crown pattern and work the top in stockinette.

9. Knit the crown. So now you've planned your top shaping and can consider its impact on

the knitting of the crown. How many rounds will the shaping take? How many inches does this translate to? Is that likely to add to the height of the hat, just cover the top of the head, or draw the existing crown section in to cover the top of the head?

Guess at proper crown depth. If your top shaping is just going to cover the top of the head, an adult hat should be maybe 5½ inches before shaping; a child's, 4½ inches. (Note that this is an off-the-table measurement: don't unroll the roll or unfold the cuff. Stand the work on the table as it will be worn and measure up to the needle.) If the top is going to draw the crown in, you may need 7 inches for an adult.

Shape top according to the plan you made in Step 8.

Add earflaps, pompoms, tassels, etc.

Ear flaps

It is simpler to add ear flaps at the end. Start the hat with about 1" of ribbing, or just in stockinette. Mark a point to be the center of each side. (It seems that ears are about in the middle from front to back, though some patterns make the two points a little closer to the back—say, 8:30 and 3:30 on a clock face where 12:00 is the wearer's nose.) Measure about 1½" to either side of the center points, and pick up 3" worth of stitches for each flap. Knit back and forth in stockinette,

decreasing 1 stitch at each end about every other row until ½ to 1" of stitches are left; bind off. Blunter, squarer flaps look more helmet-y; longer, pointier ones look more Peruvian.

If your edge all around the hat is stockinette, pick up stitches all around the hat and flaps, and add about ½" of rib or garter to keep everything flat; or do a row of single crochet. If the hat has a ribbed edge, keep the first and last 2 stitches of the ear flaps in garter stitch (i.e. knit them every row) to keep them flat. Add crocheted or twisted cord ties to the point of each flap if desired, with or without tassels or pompoms.

Pompoms

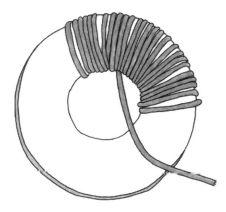

Cut 2 identical circles out of cardboard, then cut identical circles out of the center of each one, so that you have two rings. How big should each circle be? The outer circumference is approximately the total circumference of the finished

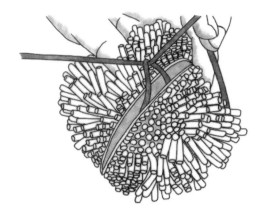

pompom. The size of the inner circle affects how plump and full the pompom will be. If the center hole is too small, you will have a fairly sparse pompom. If the center hole is too big, however, the ring may break under pressure, or the yarn tie may not be able to hold the strands securely. Probably the hole should be a little less than half the diameter of the whole disc.

Cut a *long* strand of yarn, thread it doubled through a darning needle, and start winding it around both discs held together. You don't have to do anything particular to secure the yarn ends, though they should start at the outside of the ring. Wrap yarn around and around the ring until the center is so tightly packed that you can't fit any more wraps in. When the strand is used up, cut another strand and repeat until the center is full.

Cut a 12" strand of yarn and lay it aside. Take a sharp pair of scissors and stick the point into the wrapped ball at the equator, so the point gets between the 2 cardboard discs. Cut all around the equator until every wrap has been cut. Take the 12" strand and lay it in between the discs all around the middle, then tie it as tightly as you can around the bundle of strands. Maybe wrap it again and tie another knot to be sure. Leave the ends dangling.

Pull or rip the cardboard discs away. Fluff up the pompom and trim it all around until it is even and fairly spherical, but leave the ends of the tying strand long so you can use them to attach the pompom to the hat or whatever you choose.

Chemo caps

Just about everyone knows that people undergoing chemotherapy for cancer often lose their hair, and many knitters respond by knitting hats. This is a great gesture of support, whether for your dearest friend or as an anonymous gift to a local cancer center. Pretty much any hat pattern will work, but here are some particular considerations:

Size. Subtract an inch or more from standard hat sizes, or think about a 20-inch circumference, to account for the room hair will not be taking up.

Itchiness. The skin of the scalp can be very sensitive, and a person fighting cancer doesn't need any more irritants. I recommend avoiding mohair, alpaca, angora, and even pure wool.

Warmth. This can go either way; a person without hair has lost a lot of insulation, but if the hat you're making is chiefly a fashion statement for summer or indoor wear, it may need to be very lightweight.

Washability. Again, we're talking about all-day wear next to the skin, not something that's only in use for 20 minutes in the morning and the evening. Look for something machine-washable.

Yarns I like for chemo caps: for warm ones, Plymouth Encore and Debbie Bliss Cashmerino Aran. For cool ones, Mission Falls 1824 Cotton. For dressy ones, Berroco's new Softwist. For silly ones, Sirdar Snowflake.

Where to send Chemo caps:
Ask first at your local hospital or regional cancer center. If you have no local options, you can send completed caps to:

Chemocaps
c/o Ronni Spoll
51 Sutton Place
Easton, PA 18045

For more information: Search "Chemo caps" on the web, or go to www.chemocaps.com to find patterns or learn about starting your own group to knit caps.

Decreases

k2tog

k2tog: Knit 2 together. Put the point of the right-hand needle into the next 2 sts at once, then knit them together. Slants to the right.

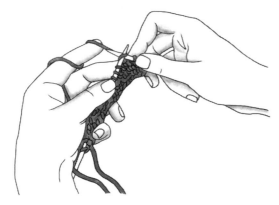

ssk A

ssk: Slip-slip-knit. Identical to the old skpsso. Insert the point of the right-hand needle into the next st as if to knit it, but slip it over without working it. (Illus. A) Do the same thing a second time. Put the point

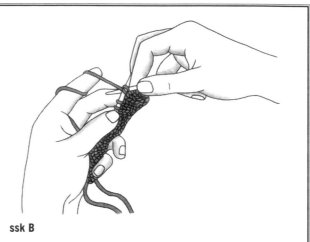

ssk B

of the left-hand needle back into both of the sts from back to front, then wrap the yarn around the tip of the right-hand needle as usual and knit the 2 together. (Illus. B) Slants to the left.

skpsso: Slip-knit-pass slipped stitch over. Identical to ssk. Insert the point of the right-hand needle into the next st as if to knit it, but slip it over without working it. Knit the next st. Use the tip of the left-hand needle to lift the slipped st over the worked st and off the end of the right-hand needle. Slants to the left.

Double decreases

k3tog: Knit 3 together. Insert the point of the right-hand needle into the next 3 sts together

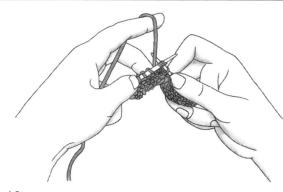

k3tog

and knit as usual. Slants to the right; the stitch that was previously on the left lands on top.

sk2p: Slip-knit2together-pass slipped stitch over. Slip next st as if to knit, knit the following 2 sts together, pass the slipped st over. Doesn't lean in either direction; the stitch that used to be on the right winds up on top.

s2kp: Slip 2-knit-pass slipped stitch over. Insert point of right-hand needle into next 2 sts together, but slip them over unworked; (Illus. A) K next st; pass the 2 slipped sts over and off the end of the right-hand needle (Illus. B). Doesn't slant; the stitch that used to be in the middle ends up on top. Also known as a centered double decrease.

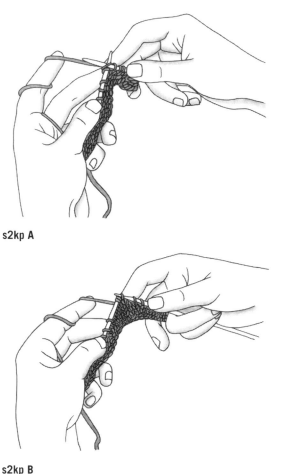

s2kp A

s2kp B

sssk: Slip-slip-slip-knit. Slip next 3 sts, one at a time, knitwise, onto right-hand needle; insert tip of left-hand needle into all 3 from back to front; wrap yarn around tip of right-hand needle and knit all 3 together. Slants left; the stitch that used to be on the right winds up on top.

Here is some space for sketching your own hat ideas.

Chapter 4

The Basics: Socks

The enormous resurgence of interest in knitting socks may have been the begining of our current enthusiasm for knitted accessories of all sorts: they're quick, fun, easy, and make great gifts. Hard to imagine now that there was a time (in the recent past!) when it seemed that double-pointed needles might disappear altogether from American knitting. I don't have to tell you why to knit socks. For *how* to knit socks, here are a few handy pointers.

Make your cast-on loose. Otherwise, it can be tough to pull the cuff over your heel, especially if you have a high instep. To keep the cast-on stitches loose but even, some knitters use a larger needle to cast on than they will use to knit the cuff or leg; others cast on over two needles held together.

Decide how the socks will be worn. Very different yarns are appropriate for shoe wear than for slipper socks or bed socks. For socks intended to wear with shoes, consider durability, thinness of fabric, and machine washability when selecting yarn; when knitting slipper or bed socks, consider warmth and softness when choosing yarn, and maybe an interesting sole pattern.

Consider reinforcing the heel and toe. The easiest way to do this is by carrying along a second strand of yarn while knitting these parts. The supplemental yarn is usually finer than the main yarn, though some knitters just double the main yarn. Almost any yarn is suitable, provided it is care-compatible with the main yarn.

Try a few different kinds of needles. Double-pointed needles are traditional for socks. If you find them inconvenient, consider what they are made of: tight knitters may prefer slippery metal

---

I know a knitter who . . .

After someone in her family received some really ugly socks for Christmas, a knitter I know got into a competition with her uncle to see who could find the craziest, most bizarre pair of socks to give the other. One year when it was her turn to give, she added eyelash and glitz and a couple nubbly novelty yarns to some scraps from her stash and knitted random stripes of random colors. Red, green, pink, brown, white—I can't even remember all the stuff that went into those socks, but believe me, they were a sight to behold.

(usually coated aluminum) needles for speed and ease, but loose knitters may have trouble keeping metal needles from falling out of the work. Loose knitters may have more success with wood or bamboo: they "grip" the yarn better.

It *is* possible to knit socks on circular needles. Some manufacturers offer a 12" circular needle, which will accommodate such a small tube (though it may not in turn accommodate most knitters' hands). Alternatively, the stitches can be divided onto two 16" circular needles, each of which is then used more-or-less like a pair of straight needles. (For more on this, see *Socks Soar on Two Circular Needles* by Cat Bordi.)

Sizing. Most sock patterns are written based on foot circumference, and they use the same measurement for the cuff and leg. This may seem ridiculous (look at your own leg; is it not bigger around than your foot?), but it works out fine surprisingly often. This is chiefly for three reasons: One, knit fabric stretches. Two, most socks don't come all the way up your calf. Three, you'd rather have a sock a little too small than a little too big, because you don't want it to fall down or bag around the ankles. So in fact, the comparison should be between the circumference of your foot and that of your ankle—usually a much closer match.

I tell you all this, as usual, to help you make whatever changes you want. Here are some guidelines for changing sock patterns.

• If your ankle is much larger or smaller than your foot: to get the right number of stitches to fit at the ankle, work the leg, heel flap, and heel on those stitches, pick up the gusset stitches as instructed, but then *change the number of decreases* worked along the gussets—for a skinnier foot, continue to decrease until you have fewer stitches than you did at the ankle; for a wider foot, decrease fewer times than the pattern instructs, and continue the foot on the remaining stitches.

• The longer you want the leg of the sock to be, the more likely you are to need more stitches, since legs get wider as you go higher up. To

Shoe size vs. length of foot

If the shoe size is...	then the foot in it measures about ...
Women's 6–7½	9¼"
Women's 8–8½	9½"
Women's 9–10; Men's 7–8	10"
Men's 9–12	11"
Men's 12½–13	11½"

Considerations when choosing yarn for socks

• Durability. Are these for hiking or for sitting in front of the fireplace?
• Washability. Who dry-cleans socks?
• Weight. Do they need to fit under shoes?
• Elasticity.
• Warmth.
• Color.

adjust, decide where you want the sock to end, then measure circumference of leg at that "altitude." Look for a size in the pattern that starts with that measurement, or just figure out how many stitches you need. (Don't forget to account for any pattern multiples when picking a cast-on number; see page 20). If you've lengthened the sock a lot, or if the wearer's ankle is much thinner than the calf, you may need to decrease stitches as you work down the leg. This is usually done at the beginning and end of the round, at the back of the leg, spread gradually over the length of the leg. It's easiest, of course, with plain stockinette stitch, so there's no pattern disruption.

• Length: If it's not convenient to measure the wearer's foot in inches, use the chart above to convert U.S. shoe size to length. Most patterns will say at the foot instructions, "Now work even until foot measures 2" less than desired total length from back of heel." This is because they think that the toe shaping is going to add 2 inches to the length of what you have already knit. This, of course, depends on what your row gauge is. At this point in the pattern, I recommend that you measure your row gauge—the number of rows in 1 inch of knitting. Then count up how many rows you will knit in following the toe instructions, and use your row gauge to see how many inches that will add to the length of your foot. For instance, if the toe shaping takes 12 rows, and you're getting about 8 rows to the inch, then the toe will only add about an inch and a half to your foot. In that case, you should keep knitting until the foot measures 1½" less than desired total length before working the toe.

A UNIVERSAL SOCK PATTERN

Have you ever used a "modular" pattern, where there are blanks in the pattern text that you fill in with the appropriate number from the chart provided? The asterisks in this pattern will guide you to the proper chart; just fill in the number of stitches based on what gauge and size you are working with.

Sizes: Adult Small (Medium, Large). Choose a size based on circumference of wearer's foot at widest point (but see notes on sizing, page 60).

Materials:
At 8 sts = 1", approx. 475 yds of yarn
At 6 sts = 1", approx. 375 yds of yarn
At 5 sts = 1", approx. 285 yds of yarn
At 4 sts = 1", approx. 200 yds of yarn
At 3½ sts = 1", approx. 150 yds of yarn
Set of 5 double-pointed needles in size to
    obtain gauge
2 safety pins or split-ring markers
Additional pin or ring marker (optional)

Cast on * sts. Divide more or less evenly onto three needles. Join into a round and work ribbing of choice (see p. 65 for some suggestions) for 1", or desired length. Change to leg pattern of choice (see p. 66 for some suggestions) and work until piece measures 6", or desired length to ankle (yardage requirements above are based on a 6" leg; for longer socks, add more yarn).

Divide for heel: Knit ** sts; turn, picking up an empty needle in the left hand, purl back across these ** sts and then purl another ** sts; these *** sts form the heel. Work back and forth on these sts in Heel Stitch, as follows:

Row 1: *With yarn in back, slip 1 stitch as if to purl; knit 1; rep from * across row. *Row 2:* With yarn in front, slip 1 stitch as if to purl, then purl remaining stitches.

Repeat Rows 1 and 2 until heel flap measures 2½", ending with Row 1. Turn heel.

Row 1: With yarn in front, slip 1 stitch as if to purl; purl ****, p2tog, turn.

Row 2: With yarn in back, slip 1 stitch as if to purl; knit *****, k2tog, turn.

Row 3: With yarn in front, slip 1 stitch as if to purl; purl *****, p2tog, turn.

Repeat Rows 2 and 3 until all stitches are absorbed into the central section, thus ending with Row 2.

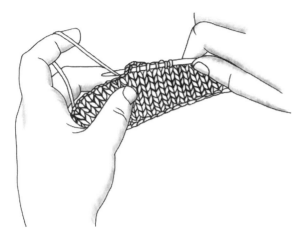

Picking up stitches

Gussets: Using an empty needle and starting at the left edge of the heel (where the working yarn is hanging), pick up and knit 1 stitch in each stitch along the left side of the heel flap. The edge stitches should be clear and somewhat elongated because they were slipped; you should have approximately 1 stitch for every 2 rows of Heel Stitch that you worked. Make a note of how many stitches you've picked up. With another empty needle, knit across all the instep stitches (These are the ones that have been ignored since the "Divide for Heel" step). To get an empty needle, you may first have to combine all the instep stitches onto the same needle—just slide them over. With another empty needle, pick up and knit 1 stitch in each stitch along the right side of the heel flap, making sure to pick up the same number you noted before.

CHART ONE FOR SOCKS:
Insert this number at "*"

GAUGE	SMALL (7" CIRC.)	MEDIUM (8" CIRC.)	LARGE (9" CIRC.)
8	56	64	72
7.5	52	60	68
7	48	56	64
6.5	44	52	60
6	40	48	56
5.5	40	44	48
5	36	40	44
4.5	32	36	40
4	28	32	36
3.5	24	28	32

CHART TWO FOR SOCKS:
Insert this number at "**"

	SMALL	MEDIUM	LARGE
8	14	16	18
7.5	13	15	17
7	12	14	16
6.5	11	13	15
6	10	12	14
5.5	10	11	12
5	9	10	11
4.5	8	9	10
4	7	8	9
3.5	6	7	8

CHART THREE FOR SOCKS:
Insert this number at "***"

	SMALL	MEDIUM	LARGE
8	28	32	36
7.5	26	30	34
7	24	28	32
6.5	22	26	30
6	20	24	28
5.5	20	22	24
5	18	20	22
4.5	16	18	20
4	14	16	18
3.5	12	14	16

CHART FOUR FOR SOCKS:
Insert this number at "*****"

	SMALL	MEDIUM	LARGE
8	16	19	22
7.5	15	18	21
7	14	16	19
6.5	12	15	18
6	11	14	16
5.5	11	12	14
5	10	11	12
4.5	8	10	11
4	7	8	10
3.5	6	7	8

CHART FIVE FOR SOCKS:
Insert this number at "******"

	SMALL	MEDIUM	LARGE
8	6	8	10
7.5	6	8	10
7	6	6	8
6.5	4	6	8
6	4	6	6
5.5	4	4	6
5	4	4	4
4.5	2	4	4
4	2	2	4
3.5	2	2	2

CHART SIX FOR SOCKS:
Insert this number at "*******"

	SMALL	MEDIUM	LARGE
8	24	24	24
7.5	20	20	24
7	20	20	20
6.5	20	20	20
6	16	16	20
5.5	16	16	16
5	12	16	16
4.5	12	12	16
4	12	12	12
3.5	12	12	12

Ribbing options for socks

Here are some options for sock cuffs. Don't overlook the possibility of using any of the mitten cuff ideas, either!

Traditional 1x1 Ribbing—Less elastic than a 2x2 ribbing, with somewhat more "grip."
Multiple of 2
Every round: (K1, p1) around.

2x2 Ribbing—Very elastic
Multiple of 4
Every round: (K2, p2) around.

3x1 Ribbing—Slightly loose
Multiple of 4
Every round: (K3, p1) around.

Mini-Cable Rib—This produces a snug ribbing with a pretty little detail

Multiple of 4
Round 1: (K2, p2) around.
Round 2: (Knit second stitch on left needle but don't slip it off; knit first stitch, then slip both off together; p2) around.
Repeat Rounds 1 and 2.

Roll Edge—Slouchy
Any number of sts
Every round: Knit.
This may also be combined with any ribbing: work the roll for ½", then proceed with rib.

Here are a few rib and rib-and-cable combinations to try out on your socks, and to get you thinking about your own unique versions.

(see p. 73 for an addition ribbing option)

Pause and take a look at what you've got: there should be four needles in the work: one with a small number of stitches and a bulge for the heel; opposite it, one with a large number of stitches for the instep or top of the foot; and one on each side connecting these two. These two "connecting" needles have the new picked-up gusset stitches. Place a safety pin or split-ring marker on the end stitch of each gusset needle that is *nearest the instep needle*—that is, the end opposite the heel. These mark the decrease points. The round now begins halfway across the short heel needle; you can mark this spot with a pin or ring marker if you like.

Shape foot: Knit across the heel sts and down the first gusset needle until 2 sts remain at the

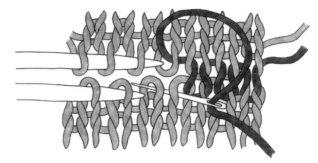

Kitchener stitch

Leg pattern options for socks

Spiral Rib
Multiple of 4
Rounds 1 and 2: (K2, p2) around.
Rounds 3 and 4: (P1, k2, p1) around.
Rounds 5 and 6: (P2, k2) around.
Rounds 7 and 8: (K1, p2, k1) around.
Repeat Rounds 1–8.

Diamond Pattern
Multiple of 4
Round 1: (K2, p1, k1) around.
Rounds 2 and 4: (K1, p1) around.
Round 3: (P1, k3) around.
Repeat Rounds 1–4.

Quaker Welt
Any number
Rounds 1–3: Knit.
Rounds 4–6: Purl.
Repeat Rounds 1–6.

original cast-on number (or desired number for foot; see notes on sizing, page 60). At this point it may be more comfortable to divide the heel stitches so that half are on each gusset needle, thus eliminating one needle. Work even on these stitches until piece measures 2" less than desired foot length, measuring from back of heel.

Shape toe: Remember those two markers that showed the gusset decrease points? If they're still in the work, take them out and move them up to the corners again—the two points where the instep needle meets the side/heel needles. This time, decrease twice at each corner, as follows: Knit to 2 sts before end of first (gusset) needle, k2tog; ssk at beginning of instep needle, knit to 2 sts before end of instep needle, k2tog; ssk at beginning of last (other gusset) needle, knit to end of round. Repeat this round until ****** sts remain all together. Knit to first corner. Cut yarn, leaving about a 24" tail. Slide all the gusset/sole stitches onto one needle. Thread tail into darning needle and graft remaining stitches using Kitchener Stitch (see above). Darn in ends.

end near the marker, K2tog. Knit across the instep needle. Ssk at the beginning (marked end) of the second gusset needle, and knit to end. This decreases 2 sts, 1 at each marked point, the "corners" where the gusset needles meet the instep. Repeat this decrease round until the total number of sts in the round is the same as the

Here is some space for sketching your own sock ideas.

Chapter 5

The Basics: Mittens

Wonderful things, mittens. They keep your hands warmer than gloves do and make you feel ready for a snowball fight at the same time. You can wear them to walk to work, to walk the dog, or to chop firewood. They are not hard to knit. To those who object that you can't wear them to drive, I say: Don't drive so much. Get out of the car, save fossil fuels, take public transportation, get some exercise, slow down, and really see your surroundings.

If you're afraid of losing a mitten, make a long old-fashioned I-cord to connect the pair to one another through the sleeves and across the back of your coat. Or make a buttonhole or button loop near the edge of each cuff, and sew a button inside the bottom of each coat sleeve.

Historically, mittens have been totally functional items to keep hands warm in winter. There are double-thumb mittens, which can be turned around when they get wet (good for shoveling snow or, so I'm told, spear-fishing); mittens lined with ultra-warm angora; "thrummed" mittens with tufts of unspun wool roving tucked between the stitches on the inside; and fulled mittens that have been washed to make them denser and warmer. But there's no need to make common sense your only guide. There are elbow-length mittens for wearing to the opera and glitzy mittens with metallic eyelash in the cuffs whose only purpose is to brighten a dull winter day.

You might think mittens present a perfect opportunity to try out a little intarsia—a snowflake on the back of the hand or a smiley face. But you can't work intarsia in the round very well, so unless you want to knit your mittens

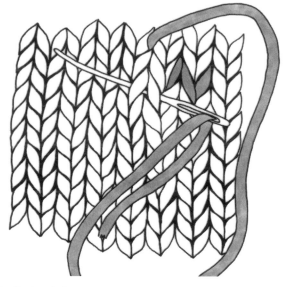

Duplicate stitch

flat and then seam them up, forget intarsia. (If you're suddenly smitten with the idea of smiley-face mittens, try duplicate stitch, illustrated above.) Instead, think fair-isle: a short stockinette cuff with a couple of little borders, a big complicated snowflake on the back with a small simple geometric all over the palm. Or try horizontal stripes or one plump cable.

Mitten design is kind of tricky because every time you turn around you're shaping the fabric again—usually, ribs at the cuff, increases for the thumb shaping, then a brief straight section, and finally decreases for the top. You can work a no-gusset thumb into the palm, but it still disrupts the pattern. One option is to work at a very fine gauge; at 8 or more stitches to the inch, you will

Two-color corrugated ribbing

This is a basic k2, p2 rib, but the knit ribs are one color and the purl ribs another. The trick (insofar as there is one) is that the yarn not in use must be carried along the back of the work—as with all stranded or fair-isle knitting. So the work proceeds this way: k2 with color A, then bring color B to the front of the work and p2; take color B back to the back of the work, and k2 with color A again. No big challenge; just don't forget and leave the B strand at the front when you go back to A (you will see your mistake quickly).

Ribbing worked this way is extremely firm; it usually draws in quite a bit and has almost none of the elasticity of single-color ribbing. It's very traditional for the borders of fair-isle garments and provides a nice way of continuing the colors all the way out to the edges of the piece.

have enough stitches across the back for some serious patterning. Another is to knit plain and embellish afterwards: embroidered or appliquéd knitted leaves, for instance. Or add a bobble here and there as you knit, with a bobble edge at the cuff (see page 75). Try some stress-free beads or sequins: string them on the yarn before you start,

Cabled band (see p. 65 for additional ribbing options)

Yarn considerations for mittens

- Warmth.
- Durability.
- Softness, unless the mittens will be worn over another pair of gloves or mittens.
- Washability, if for children or outdoor work.

NUMBER OF STITCHES TO CAST ON WHEN KNITTING MITTENS:

GAUGE	WOMEN'S S 7"	WOMEN'S M/MEN'S S 8"	WOMEN'S L/MEN'S M 9"	MEN'S L 10"
3	20	24	28	30
3.5	24	28	32	36
4	28	32	36	40
4.5	32	36	40	44
5	36	40	46	50
5.5	38	44	50	54
6	42	48	54	60
7	50	56	64	70
8	56	64	72	80

and slide them up between stitches wherever you want them (but not on the palm!).

BASIC MITTEN PATTERN

Here is a simple outline to use as a jumping-off point for your own mitten designs. For sizing, measure around palm of hand above thumb.

Materials:
For Women's Medium, approximately 130
    yards at 3.5 sts per inch; 150 yds at 5
    sts per inch; 175 yds at 6 sts per inch.
set of 4 or 5 double-pointed needles in
    size to obtain gauge
2 stitch markers
stitch holder

Note: When checking your gauge, note your vertical gauge (how many *rows* per inch of knitting) as well as your horizontal gauge (how many stitches).

Cast on the correct number of stitches (see chart on page 73). Join and work in the round in cuff pattern of your choice (see Chapter 4 for suggestions, page 65) for 2–3".

Change to stockinette or the stitch pattern of your choice and work ¼" to ½" without shaping.

Shape thumb gusset: Knit to 1 stitch before the middle of the round (for left mitten) or 1 stitch after (for right mitten). Place marker on either side of this stitch. Increase on each side of marked stitch, but inside the markers (now is a good time for the m1, or "make 1," increase, see page 76). Knit to end of round.

If your row gauge is 3.5 rows = 1" or less, continue to increase 1 stitch on each side inside the markers (that is, right after the first marker and right before the second). If your row gauge is more than 3.5 to the inch, work one round plain, and then alternate an increase round with a plain round. In either case, increase until the number of stitches between the markers is one-quarter of the original cast-on number (or a little more if you need to round off). Then knit one round plain.

On the next round, knit to the first marker and remove it. Slip the stitches from between the markers (these are the gusset stitches) onto a stitch holder. Onto the right-hand needle, cast on stitches to replace the gusset stitches—1 stitch if your gauge is 4 or fewer stitches to the inch, 3 stitches if your gauge is more. (If you are working any kind of pattern that makes 1 new stitch, or 2, better than 3 or vice versa, cast on that number instead. The difference isn't that important to the fit.)

Now continue to work in the round until the hand is nearly as long as it needs to be—the top decreases happen pretty quickly, particularly in the bulkier gauges, and they can easily make the mitten feel too short. I would stop when the work reaches ¼" from the top of my longest finger, or maybe ½" if my gauge is 5 stitches to the inch or more.

Shape top: Begin by adjusting the number of stitches to be convenient with the rest of the top shaping. If your total number isn't divisible by 5, work one round with some randomly-placed decreases to bring it into line. Now, divide the remaining number by 5; for a moment, we'll call the result "n."

For your first "real" decrease round, knit n–2 stitches (whatever "n" is, minus 2 stitches), then k2tog; repeat this 4 more times, which should bring you right to the end of the round. Next, knit n–3 stitches, then k2tog, and repeat *that* 4 times around. The next round begins with n–4, then n–5, etc. When your total number of stitches is down to 10 or fewer (for gauges of 3.5 to the inch and less) or 16 or so for finer gauges, finish off. Cut the yarn (leaving about 6"), thread it through the remaining stitches (twice for added security), and fasten off.

Now the thumb: Go back to the hole where the stitches are on the holder. At the upper edge of the hole are the cast-on stitch or stitches. Turn the mitten upside-down and pick up 3 stitches along that little cast-on edge (for picking up stiches, see illustration on p. 63). Slip the stitches from the holder back onto 2 needles (dividing roughly in half), and knit in the round on these

Bobble edging

To make a bobble, work (k1, p1, k1, p1, k1) all into one stitch, then turn and k5, turn again and p5, turn again and k5; finally, turn once more, p5, then pass 4th, 3rd, 2nd, and 1st stitch over last stitch and off the end of the needle.

Cast on desired number, preferably a multiple of 5.

Round 1: p2, *make bobble, p4; rep from * to end of round.

Rounds 2 and 3: Purl.

Continue with any other cuff pattern you like.

stitches until the thumb is nearly as long as your thumb. The thumb decreases happen even faster than the top: start with (k2, k2tog), then (k1, k2tog); then k2tog all the way around if you still have more than 10 stitches—otherwise just fasten off.

Increases

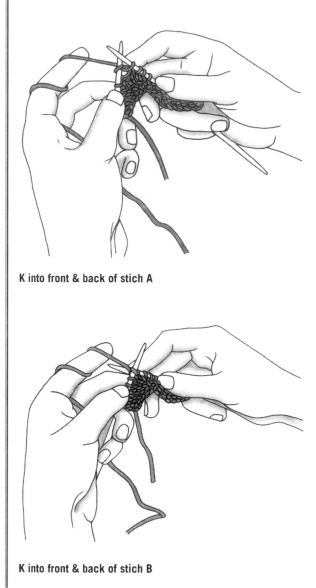

K into front & back of stich A

K into front & back of stich B

K into front and back of stitch: This is what it sounds like. Knit into the stitch the way you usually do, but don't let the old stitch off the left-hand needle (Illus. A); instead, bring the point of the right-hand needle around and into the back of the stitch, and knit it again (Illus. B). Presto—two stitches from one.

K and p into same stitch: Start as above, by knitting the stitch but leaving it on the needle. Now bring the yarn forward between the points of the needles, insert the right-hand needle into the stitch purlwise, and purl it. Again, two stitches from one.

M1, "make one": If you look closely at the space between the last stitch on the right-hand needle and the first stitch on the left-hand needle, you'll see a piece of yarn or "bar." Bring the tip of the left-hand needle up under this strand from behind (Illus. A). Insert the right-hand needle into it knitwise (thus forcing it to twist), and knit it as usual (Illus. B). A new stitch has emerged from nowhere.

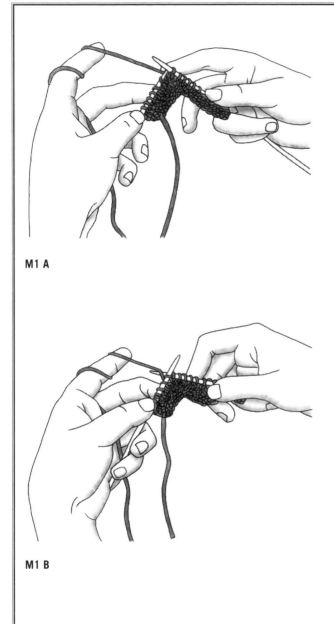

M1 A

M1 B

M1L: Close examination of the m1 increase might reveal that its base slants a little to the right. If you would like an increase to mirror that one and lean a little to the left, insert the tip of the left needle under the strand *from front to back,* and then knit the strand through the *back* of the loop.

There are two chief differences between increases #1 and #2, and increases #3 and #4. The first is that #1 and #2 produce increased stitches that look like purls—the new stitch has a little bar across its base, which may seem disruptive in a stockinette fabric. #3 and #4 don't have this problem. The second is that #1 and #2 both take place in a stitch, and turn one stitch into two, while #3 and #4 take place between stitches and create a stitch as if from nowhere. Neither is superior, but it's important to consider the difference if you're substituting one kind of increase for another in a pattern: your stitch count may not be right otherwise.

How to make a ruffle

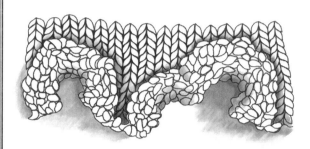

Fabrics ruffle when one edge of something is much, much wider than the other. In sewing, this effect is usually achieved by cutting a wide strip of fabric and gathering one long edge in (often with a basting thread). In knitting, where we create the fabric as we go, there are two possibilities: start with a wide fabric and then decrease rapidly, or start with a narrow fabric and increase rapidly.

You can put a ruffle at the edge of almost any stockinette fabric. Just bear in mind that the fabric has to be soft to ruffle well. If the main fabric is firm, as with mittens or socks, switch to larger needles for the ruffle to loosen it up a bit.

Ruffle at the beginning (cast-on) edge:
Loosely cast on 4 times the number of stitches called for by the finished item—e.g. for a sock that's going to use 60 stitches around

the leg, cast on 240. Working in stockinette, work 1 row or round. Next row or round: work 2 together all the way across/around. Third: Repeat the second. Now you're down to the original number, and you have a little curly ruffle at the edge. (Note for knitting in the round: four times the usual number is probably too many stitches for your double-pointed or circular needle, and when the stitches are crowded, it's very hard to be sure you've joined without twisting. You may prefer to knit the ruffle part flat, then join the work into a round when the decreasing is finished; you can use the cast-on tail later to sew up the short seam.)

Ruffle at the end (bind-off) edge:
Row/Round 1: Working in stockinette, increase in every stitch. Row/Round 2: Repeat #1. Row/Round 3: Work even. Row/Round 4: Bind off *loosely.* You will probably prefer the look of a "make 1" increase rather than any of the "work twice into the same stitch" increases. Since the m1 is worked between stitches, however, you won't quite double the number of stitches each time if you're working back and forth: 60 stitches have only 59 spaces between them. No big deal.

Some pretty fair-isle borders

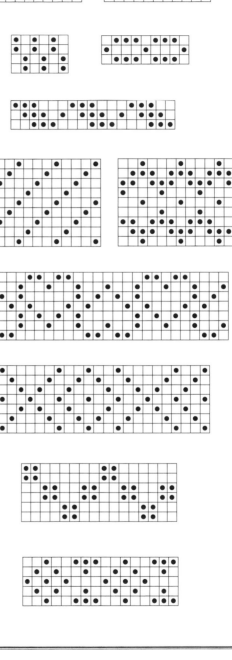

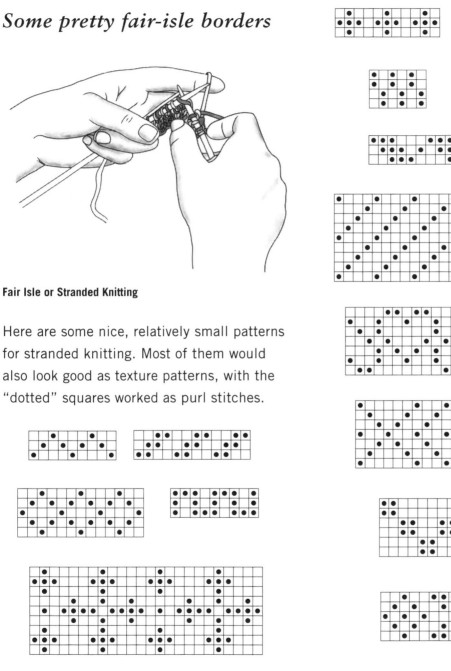

Fair Isle or Stranded Knitting

Here are some nice, relatively small patterns for stranded knitting. Most of them would also look good as texture patterns, with the "dotted" squares worked as purl stitches.

Here is some space for sketching your own mitten ideas.

Chapter 6

The Basics: Scarves

As I write this, scarves are *the* accessory to have. This is excellent news for knitters, of course, as they are also quick and easy to make. And one can never have too many: One for each coat or jacket, obviously, but also some that are lighter and others that are toasty warm. For my own trench coat, I rotate among several scarves, depending on the weather and the occasion. There's a very warm silk/wool blend, short enough to tuck the ends inside the open neck of the coat; a nearly shawl-sized triangle knit of fine mohair on a large needle that keeps the rain off my head but stays light and airy; a tiny "neck cozy" of unspun silk that I can crumple and shove in a pocket. And I think I'll need another this season, something long and skinny in an attention-getting yarn.

It's good to have scarves to coordinate with favorite suits for indoor wear as well. The perfect scarf to jazz up a simple dress doesn't always have to be a printed silk square; it can be a unique yarn knit long and skinny or in a triangle.

And if *you* can never have too many scarves, it follows that the same is true of your nearest and dearest. (And frankly, scarves can be simple enough to give as gifts to the less-near and less-dear.) This chapter has instructions for a wide variety of stitches and structures, but the simplest scarves don't need a pattern at all. Probably the first real "thing" you ever knit was a scarf. Scarves are great beginner projects because they do not require any shaping. They don't, in fact, need anything but a knit stitch. Garter stitch makes a good scarf because it is reversible and makes a fabric that lies flat rather than rolling or curling at the edges. If you used a plain yarn—

maybe someone's leftovers in a color you hadn't chosen and didn't love—that first scarf may have felt like homework: boring, interminable, pointless. But the new garter-stitch scarves are entirely different animals. They use large needles and require only a few stitches, either for a very narrow lacy fabric or because the yarn is huge. For scarves like this, plan to cast on between 10 and 15 stitches on needles size US #15, 17, or 19.

How to choose which needles and how many stitches? Well, of course you know by now that my answer is going to be, "Swatch several ways, and see what you like," but I'll give you a pass this time. It really doesn't matter that much. Larger needles produce larger stitches, but for wide, open, meshy fabrics, the difference won't be all that noticeable. Use whichever needles you have on hand.

For more traditional scarves, here are some guidelines:

Width. Men's scarves seem typically to be about 7 inches wide, going to 8 inches or even 9 inches for wide scarves for casual wear. Standard women's scarves used to be about 8 inches wide, but that is shrinking a bit lately; the fashionable thin ones might be as narrow as 6 inches, 5 inches, or even 4 inches. For a woman's shawl, think about a minimum of a 14-inch width, with 18–22 inches more typical.

In any consideration of width, you must take the thickness of the fabric into account. Bulkier fabrics have less drape and so will not fold as easily at the back of the neck or under the chin; keep these scarves narrower so the wearer won't feel smothered or choked.

Length. A man's dressy scarf, meant to go behind the neck and then have the ends overlap under a coat, might be as short as 30 inches. Typical "standard" length for men's scarves is 66–72 inches, which is enough go around behind the neck, circle round the front and behind the neck again, and down the other side with reasonable length at each end. For people who request "really long" scarves, consider their height, how many times they're going to wrap it around their neck, and how silly they will look if it habitually gets caught between their legs.

Women's scarves might start at 42 inches to go under the lapels of a blazer; 60 inches is a pretty common standard length.

You will have to think about thickness and drape of fabric when deciding on length, too. Thick fabrics can't necessarily be wound around the neck an extra time to take up extra length.

Finally, remember to include any planned fringe as part of the total length.

How much yarn? Ballpark estimates used to say 300–400 yards was a good minimum for a scarf, but this is now both too much and too little. The yarn called "Rayon Fluff" from Great Adirondack Yarn Co. has 82 yards in a skein, and 1 skein makes a great short scarf if you use

US #13 needles, cast on 13 stitches, and knit in garter stitch until the yarn runs out. This is a good typical example for loosely knit fabrics on very big needles.

On the other hand, an 8-inch-wide, 60-inch-long scarf knit in garter stitch with a worsted-weight yarn on #8 needles could, in my experience, easily need 450–500 yards of yarn. (Note that this is higher than the "Ballpark Yardage" chart in Chapter 2 would suggest because garter stitch takes more rows than stockinette does to cover the same distance.) And if you're working with finer yarns or adding cables or other yarn-intensive stitches, you'll need proportionally more. Fringe or tassels will add a surprising amount to the yarn requirements: for a 6-inch fringe on an 8-inch-wide scarf, you might need 30 extra yards.

Choosing a stitch. There are two chief things to keep in mind:

1. Both sides of the fabric will probably be visible at various times, so choose something that doesn't look bad on the reverse. For me, this means no fair-isle, no intarsia, and no typical cables. Lots of ribs work well, though, as do most knit-purl combinations and most garter-based lace patterns.

2. Flat is better than sausage-shaped for a scarf. Resist the urge to do stockinette stitch, as it will roll up at all the edges. Knitters plead with me almost daily ("Couldn't I just put a little garter at the edges to keep it flat?" or "What if I knit very loosely?") and then later they plead with me to fix it ("Couldn't I just press it really well?" or, "What if I crochet around it?"). Stockinette curls. Nothing will fix that. There are millions of alternatives, and you can learn to love them.

BIAS-KNIT SCARF

This works with pretty much any yarn, and looks especially good in a space-dyed one.

Yarn considerations for scarves

- Softness—no itchies here!
- Warmth.
- Drape. Consider using a slightly larger needle than usual for a softer fabric.
- Washability.
- Pattern clarity.
- Color.
- Allergies.

Note that this is maybe the only time you can ignore durability if you want to—*this* is the spot for those lovely fragile cashmeres, alpacas, and novelties that your local shop owner or knitting guru keeps telling you won't hold up in socks.

Cast on 2 sts. *Row 1:* Inc in each st. *Row 2:* Knit. *Row 3:* Inc in first stitch, knit to last stitch, increase in last stitch. Repeat rows 2 and 3 until the length of the 2 edges that aren't on the needle equals desired width of scarf, ending with Row 2.

Next row: Inc in first st, k to last 2 sts, k2tog. *Next row:* Knit. Repeat last 2 rows until length of longest side equals desired length of scarf, ending with a plain knit row.

Next row: K2tog, k to last 2 sts, k2tog. *Next row:* Knit. Repeat last 2 rows until 2 sts remain. K2tog; fasten off.

MONDO CABLE

This scarf is an exception to my no-cables rule. It makes use of Lily Chin's "ribble" technique to produce one huge, reversible braid. Because it is both ribbed and cabled, it can get very bulky; the most suitable yarns are light, airy mohair-type yarns like Berroco's Mohair Classic or Artful Yarns' Portrait.

Cast on 24 sts. (In theory, any multiple of 6 sts will work, though I don't recommend fewer than 18 or more than 30. In any case, adjust rows 12 and 24 so that ⅓ of the total sts are placed on the cable needle each time. Experiment with working more or fewer rows between cable twists.)

All rows except rows 12 and 24: (K1, p1) across.

Row 12: (K1, p1) 4x; slip next 8 sts to cable needle and hold at back of work; (k1, p1) 4x; (k1, p1) across sts from cable needle.

Row 24: Slip 8 sts to cable needle and hold at front of work; (k1, p1) 4x; (k1, p1) across sts from cable needle; (k1, p1) to end of row.

Repeat these 24 rows for desired length. Bind off on row 11 or row 23.

LENGTHWISE STRIPES

You don't have to cast on at one end and knit hundreds of rows: you can work a scarf from side to side. This makes it easy to put in vertical stripes.

Decide on a desired length (before fringe). Multiply this by your stitch gauge. Cast on this number (you'll probably want a 24-inch or longer circular needle to accommodate the large number of stitches). Work in garter stitch throughout, or

MESH STITCH

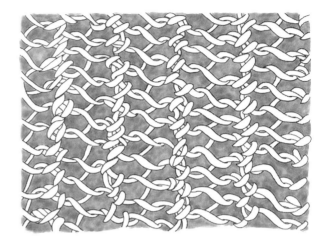

work 10 or more rows of garter at the cast-on and bind-off edges, plus 5 or more stitches of garter at the beginning and end of each row, and the rest in stockinette.

You can work regular stripes by changing colors at planned intervals, or switch yarns randomly, or combine both by improvising for the first half and then mirroring the same sequence back to the bind-off edge. This is also a great spot for a variegated yarn that changes colors slowly, like Kureyon or Silk Garden from Noro. If you are working in garter, you will probably want to designate one side as the "good" side and only change colors at the beginning of "good"-side rows. Otherwise, you'll see a row of interlocking dots and dashes of the new color with the old color—which, on the other hand, you may decide you like.

This is a little more elegant than just working garter stitch on huge needles to get a lacy effect. It still requires a fairly large needle—say, US #11 for a worsted-weight yarn—and fairly few stitches for the desired width.

Cast on any even number of stitches. Every row is worked the same way: P1, (yo, p2tog) to last st, p1.

You may ask yourself: Why p2tog? Why not lots of k2tog instead? The answer has to do with where the purl-side bumps turn up; try it and see. You can get the same effect by working k1, (ssk, yo) to last st, k1, but all that slipping really slows you down.

STOCKINETTE TUBE

This only works if you want a really thick scarf or are willing to work on really thin yarn, but it will give you a stockinette scarf with no ugly wrong side and no curling problem.

Using a 16-inch circular needle, cast on a number of stitches equal to twice the desired width of the scarf. Join, being careful not to twist, and work in the round in stockinette as long as desired—in stripes or fair-isle patterning if you like (though stranding two yarns will thicken the scarf yet again). Bind off. Flatten the tube so that the beginning of the round becomes one side edge, and sew both ends shut.

SLIP-STITCH PATTERN

This stitch uses two different yarns to produce a reversible fabric: one side has ribs in color A, the other side in B. You can choose two colors of the same yarn, but it can also be fun to use two different yarns, as long as both are roughly the same weight—maybe one solid and one multicolor, or one nubby with one that is smooth, or one a little fuzzy with one that has a little sparkle. Yarn requirements for this aren't double what they would be for a plain scarf, but they are greater; so allow maybe 25% more yardage.

Cast on a multiple of 10 sts, plus 3 more.

Row 1: With Yarn A, k3, *slip 2 sts with yarn in front, k8; rep from * to end of row.

Row 2: With Yarn A, *k3, p2, k3, slip 2 sts with yarn in back; rep from * to last 3 sts; k3.

Row 3: With Yarn B, repeat Row 2.

Row 4: With Yarn B, repeat Row 1.

Repeat these 4 rows for desired length; bind off.

DROP-STITCH LOZENGE PATTERN

This isn't exactly reversible, but it is pretty on both sides. A yarn that's a little bit fuzzy will look and feel nice, though you'll probably have to "encourage" the stitches to drop by tugging or fussing at them a little bit once the scarf is finished.

Start with any multiple of 8 sts plus 4 more; after the foundation row, the pattern is worked on a multiple of 9 plus 4.

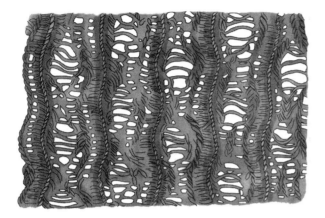

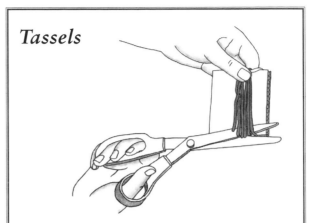

Tassels

Foundation Row: K1, (p2, k1, yo, k1, p2, k2) to last 3 sts, p2, k1.

Rows 1, 3, and 5: P1, (k2, p2, k2, p3) to last 3 sts, k2, p1.

Rows 2 and 4: K1, (p2, k3, p2, k2) to last 3 sts, p2, k1.

Row 6: K1, (p2, k1, drop next st from needle and allow it to ravel back to the previous yo, k1, p2, k1, yo, k1) to last 3 sts, p2, k1.

Rows 7, 9, and 11: P1, (k2, p3, k2, p2), rep to last 3 sts, k2, p1.

Rows 8 and 10: K1, (p2, k2, p2, k3) to last 3 sts, p2, k1.

Row 12: K1, (p2, k1, yo, k1, p2, k1, drop next st from needle and allow it to ravel back to the previous yo, k1) to last 3 sts, p2, k1.

Rep rows 1 through 12 for desired length, ending with Row 5 or Row 11. For concluding row, drop middle st of "k3" set but do not work new yo's. Bind off in rib.

Cut a piece of cardboard 3 or 4" wide and as tall as you want your tassel to be. Cut a 12" strand of yarn and lay it along the top edge of the cardboard; this will be your tying strand. Wind yarn around and around the cardboard, over the tying strand. How many times you wind the yarn depends on how thick you want your tassel to be. Cut the yarn.

Pick up the ends of the tying strand and tie them as tightly as you can around the bundle of strands at the top. With sharp scissors, cut the strands along the bottom edge of the cardboard.

Now cut a 24" strand of yarn as a binding thread. Leave 6 or 8" sticking out, and wind around and around the "neck" of the tassel right below the top tie. Tie the two ends of the binding strand together and use a darning needle to poke them through the binding, into the middle of the tassel, and out the bottom. Trim all the ends even.

Fringe

Almost everything about fringe is a matter of taste. The usual thing is not to attach strands in every stitch, but to put clusters of 2–4 strands in every second or third stitch. But you can put big fringe at 1-inch intervals, or have sparse fringe lying smoothly side by side, just as it is your decision whether to do a little 1½-inch fringe or a luxurious 8 inches. In any case, here's how to do the math:

First, calculate the length of each strand. If the fringe is going to hang 5 inches below the end of the scarf, you'll need twice 5 inches plus 1 inch to be used up in the knot that holds it onto the scarf: Thus you would cut strands that were each 11 inches long. (Consider cutting 11½ or 12 inches, since you will probably want to trim the ends even.)

Second, calculate the number of strands. The easiest way to judge this is to cut several strands and attach them to the edge of the scarf to see what works best in terms of number of strands per cluster and spacing of clusters. Once you have decided this, multiply the number of clusters you'll have across the edge by the number of strands per cluster—then double that, since you will need fringe for both ends of the scarf.

Cut the fringe. Do not sit with a ruler or tape measure and measure each strand. Just as you would do when making a tassel (see page 93), cut a piece of cardboard as wide as half your strand length; that is, for the 5-inch fringe in the example above, make the cardboard 5½ or 6 inches wide. Wind the yarn around and around the cardboard, being careful not to stretch the yarn and trying to keep the wraps lying neatly next to each other. Count as you wind.

If you need many more strands than will fit across the cardboard template, consider doing half at a time, because once the template is covered with yarn, each wrap around it is longer than the ones in the previous layer. This is increasingly wasteful as time passes, since you'll always have to trim the finished fringe to the length of the shortest strand. Finally, cut the yarn from the ball, and then cut along *one* long edge of the template to separate the strands from each other.

Attach the fringe. Take the requisite number of strands for one cluster, hold them together, and fold them in half. Working from the wrong side of the fabric, insert a crochet hook through the edge of the scarf and pull the midpoint of the

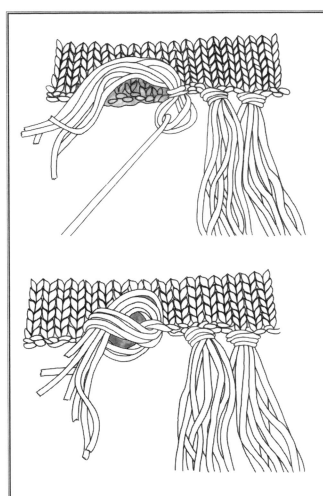

straighten the fringe so it lies neatly, place a straight edge over it as a cutting guide, and cut away the uneven ends. You may want to place old newspaper on your flat surface before you start to catch the millions of tiny bits you'll create.

Variations. If you have any experience with macramé, you can tie a second and even a third row of knots to join the groups of fringe to one another in a net pattern. You can also put beads on the ends of the fringe: Start with a completed fringe, then thread each end of yarn through a bead (a beading needle may help) and tie a simple overhand knot to keep the bead in place.

Consider using a contrasting color for fringe, or even a different yarn. Or make the fringe out of various different colors and widths of ribbon to coordinate with a multicolor yarn.

If you don't like fringe, you might want to make a few pompoms and attach them at the corners, or at the corners and midpoint of each side. See page 51 for pompom making instructions.

cluster through to form a loop, as in the illustration.

Pass all the ends of the cluster through the loop, and snug the knot up to the edge of the scarf. Repeat for all the other clusters along both ends of the scarf.

Trim the fringe. You can do it by eye, or you can lay the scarf on a flat surface,

Here is some space for sketching your own scarf ideas.

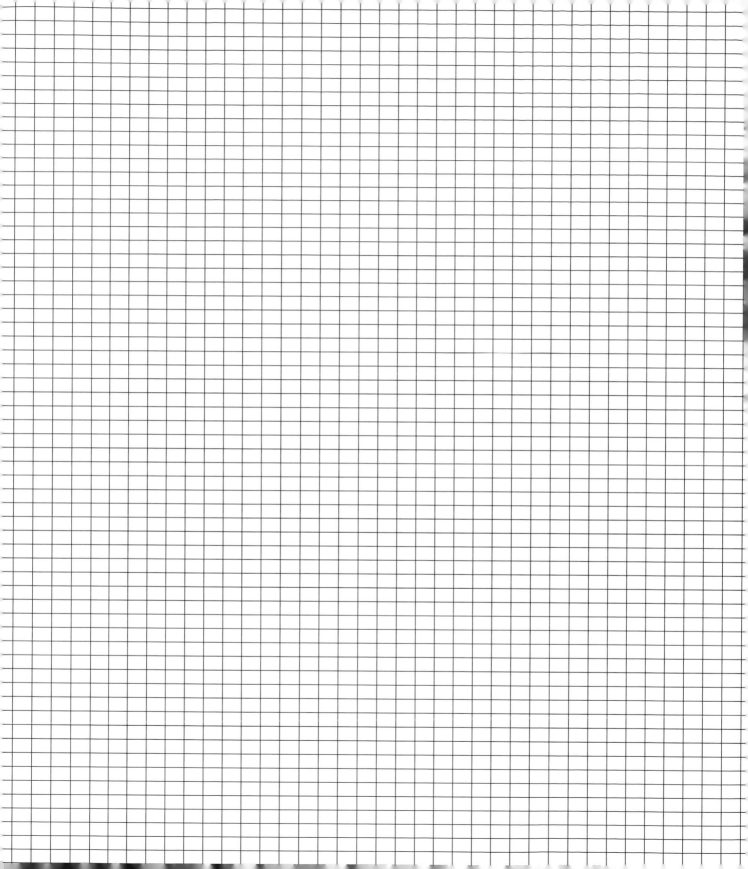

Chapter 7

The Basics: Bags

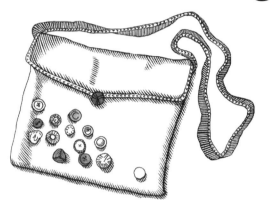

Until recently they were the most overlooked of knitted accessories. But bags offer knitters much the same blank canvas that scarves do: no worries about fit, no need to use the same one every day, no huge investment of time or money. Add to that more freedom of design (no issues of reversibility, no worrying that a particular color is unflattering near the wearer's face), and you've got a world of possibilities.

Compared to bags, hats look generic and scarves are all the same. Bags offer variety. There are purses and handbags—clutches, shoulder straps, drawstring pouches—but there are also knitted backpacks, string bags for marketing, totes, and even knitted knitting bags. You can make beaded evening bags, amulet pouches, or felted hobo bags. Take your inspiration from distant times and places, like Victorian reticules or woven straw beach bags from South America. Remember the open-topped shoulder bags from the early 1970s that we called Indian because their fabric reminded us of Native American weaving? What about the velvet or tapestry bag that holds a *tallit,* the Jewish prayer shawl? Or the original eighteenth-century "pocket," the forerunner of today's fanny pack, which was a small bag tied around the waist like an apron? All of these have great knitting potential.

As you plan a bag, your toughest choice is the yarn. People have a tendency to put things in bags, and knitting has a tendency to stretch; the

Yarn considerations for bags

• Strength. Does it lack stretch?
• Durability. Is it resistant to abrasion?
• Color.
• Fiber. For felted bags, only animal fibers will work: primarily wool, mohair, and alpaca, though also cashmere (but what a waste!), angora, camel hair, dog hair, etc.

combination presents some challenges. Unless you want to line the bag with fabric (which is always an option) you'll want a fabric that's sturdy enough to hold its shape and dense enough to keep something like keys from poking through. This is one of the few moments when I'm not going to make a pitch for wool. Cottons hold their shape well, especially if they're knitted fairly tightly, and even more so if they're blended with some acrylic (also known as microfiber). Linen (or flax) is also very sturdy and durable, as are raw silks (the shiny, silky-looking ones seem in my experience more likely to fray, however).

Mohair is in a category by itself. Its most common form for knitting yarn is the soft, fluffy, brushed style; if this is what you think of, you'll probably expect it to be fragile. But mohair is in fact quite strong. The hairy, brushed mohair yarns will hold up to use in a bag, provided you knit them tightly enough to keep holes from

being an issue. (Maybe stranding a mohair with a plain yarn for density would solve the problem.) If you're lucky, though, you'll find mohair yarns that *aren't* fluffy. When blended with wool and spun tightly into a conventional twisted yarn, mohair gives luster, strength, and durability, without the fuzzy look. There aren't many of these on the market (R.I.P. Classic Elite's "Tapestry"); Green Mountain Spinnery has a good one in "Mountain Mohair." Rowan's modestly fuzzy Kid Classic isn't a bad choice either.

Of course, there is one kind of bag where wool and its soft, fine cousins like alpaca and angora are necessities: felted ones. If you knit a loose fabric and deliberately full it (usually by shrinking it in a washing machine), the result will be as dense and durable as you'd wish. Bags are great projects for experimenting with felting, because exact finished size isn't crucial. While you're getting to know your yarns and your washer, you can be making hosts of quick, unique items for gifts.

Bags may in fact make better gifts even than scarves. They're certainly a great option for the wool-averse or wool-allergic. They aren't kept next to the skin, and they knit up beautifully in cotton and other non-wool yarns. I know brides who have knit dressy evening bags as gifts for their bridesmaids, and one knitter who made matching bags, coordinated to the bridesmaids' dresses, for all of the female members of the wedding party to carry at the event. This was so successful that she almost regretted it: friends and family members began to request that she outfit *their* wedding parties, too.

Having chosen a yarn, you need to choose a fabric. Plain ol' stockinette is great here, or something with one or more cables, since cables thicken and tighten the fabric. Slip-stitch patterns are great for the same reason. Lace is best avoided, unless you plan to line the finished bag (white on white for a wedding, perhaps, or red satin behind black for evening?). As always, swatching is the way to get information, more about texture and hand this time than about size.

For the moment, I'm going to assume that your desired bag is either rectangular or can be broken down into a number of rectangular shapes. The easiest bag is made by knitting a rectangle, then folding it in half the short way and sewing two sides closed. Leave the top open, or crochet a button loop, or sew on a toggle. The next-easiest bag folds that same rectangle in thirds for an envelope-style clutch (another closure option: I-cord frogs, or a snap under the flap).

Feeling more ambitious? For approximately the last third of the knitting, decrease at both ends of the row to produce a pointed flap. Ready for a gusset? Fold your rectangle into a fairly narrow "U" shape, and knit two narrow rectangular panels, one to sew in each side. Some bags are made of two identical rectangles, one each

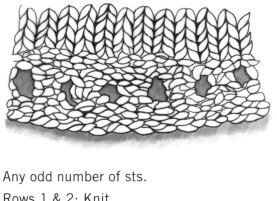

Edging a Bag

This makes a pretty edging for a fold-over bag, and has the advantage of giving you buttonholes anywhere you might want them.

Any odd number of sts.
Rows 1 & 2: Knit
Row 3: (k2tog, yo) to last st k1.
Row 4: Knit

for front and back, plus a *long* narrow strip that is sewn along three edges of each of the panels, then goes up over the wearer's shoulder and back down to meet its own beginning.

See how easy this is? Think of the front and back of the bag as your canvas, and sketch out some ideas. If you are thinking about a cable, do you want one big one in the middle, or three evenly spaced across? Or an allover cable lattice pattern? Or one cable placed asymmetrically? Bags are pretty small, compared to sweaters; you'll want to plan out the spacing of various elements in advance. Otherwise, you're liable to find that the cable only crosses twice—once hidden by the flap, and once almost at the fold at the bottom.

Basic bag design, though, is elementary math: if I want the finished bag about 9″ wide, how many stitches will I need to make 9″? Does this stitch pattern require a multiple of 4? Fine, I'll subtract 1 stitch and cast on 44 instead of 45.

Bags, like pillows, are a terrific moment for intarsia, the color technique used for pictorial motifs. You can place your design without considering whether the sweater's shaping will interfere, and you do not have to worry about all the ends on the inside showing. Outline the bag on a piece of graph paper, and then play around with the size, shape, and placement of your design. Charts for a few simple motifs, and a quick refresher illustration of how to work intarsia patterns, are at right and below, respectively.

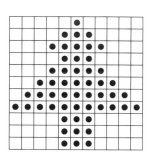

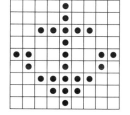

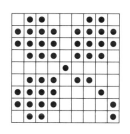

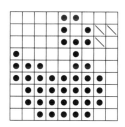

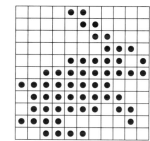

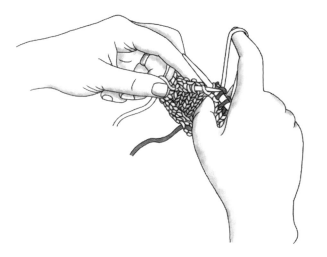

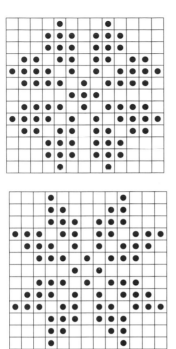

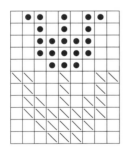

The rest of this chapter has two parts: instructions for a basic felted bag, in case you've never done any felted knitting before, and ideas for various embellishments. Most of the embellishments will work on plain or fulled bags, on stockinette or reverse-stockinette fabrics. This is the fun of knitting your own: when you make it yourself, you can make it unique.

FELTED BAG

Finished Size: Who knows? That's the adventure of felting. Not very big, in any event: maybe 6" wide at the base.

Materials:

Approx. 200 yards of wool yarn, not superwash (Superwash yarns have been treated to prevent shrinkage, which is exactly the point of felting)

16" circular needle, US #10½

2 US #10½ double-pointed needles for I-cord straps (optional)

5 stitch markers

Gauge: About 3 sts = 1" over stockinette (Exact gauge is not important, as long as the knitting is quite loose.)

Base: Cast on 12 sts. Work back and forth in garter stitch for 48 rows; strip should be about 8" long. Continuing on from the end of the last

Slip-stitch patterns for bags

All of these are particularly interesting in variegated yarns. Also, try using two different yarns, alternating 2 rows of one with 2 rows of the other.

Linen Stitch
Any even number of stitches.
Row 1: K1, *slip 1 st with yarn in front, k1; rep from * to last st, k1.
Rows 2 and 4: K1, p to last st, k1.
Row 3: K1, *k1, slip 1 st with yarn in front; rep from * to last st, k1.
Repeat these 4 rows.

Bird's Eye Stitch
Any even number of stitches.
Row 1: K1, *slip 1 st with yarn in back, k1; rep from * to last st, k1.
Rows 2 and 4: K1, p to last st, k1.
Row 3: K1, *k1, slip 1 st with yarn in back; rep from * to last st, k1.
Repeat these 4 rows.

Fabric Stitch
Any odd number of stitches.
Row 1: K1, *slip 1 st with yarn in front, k1; rep from *.
Row 2: K1, *p1, slip 1 st with yarn in back; rep from * to last st, k1.
Repeat these 2 rows.

row, pick up and knit 24 sts along the side edge of the strip—1 stitch in each garter ridge. Pick up and knit 12 sts along cast-on edge of base, and 24 sts along other long edge: 72 sts total.

Body: Continue working in the round, placing a marker to show the beginning of the round. Place markers for corners as follows: K1, *pm, k10, pm, k26, rep from * once to end of round, ending k25. Next round: *K to marker, slip marker, slip next st with yarn in back, rep from * to end of round. Next round: Knit. Repeat these two rounds until piece measures about 9" from base. Bind off. Weave in ends.

Straps: You can sew leather, ribbon, or fabric straps to the finished bag, or you can knit felt ones, as follows. Using dpn, cast on 4 sts. *Do not turn work. Slide sts to other end of needle, pull yarn behind needle to beginning of row, and k4. Rep from * until strap measures 12". Bind off; weave in ends. Make second strap the same.

Fulling the bag: Set your washing machine on lowest water level and hottest temperature. Put the knitted piece(s) into a zipper pillowcase. Add a little detergent to the water, and maybe a couple old towels if you have them. Having more stuff in the washer speeds the process up. Later, when you're an old hand at this, you will be knitting and fulling half a dozen items at a time, which will serve the same purpose. Check on the bag every five minutes or so, by stopping the washer, fishing out the pillowcase, and opening it to see if the bag has begun to shrink. As soon as you see any change, start checking more frequently; every two minutes isn't too often. If the wash cycle finishes and the washer wants to drain and rinse, don't let it: set it back for further agitation. (If your machine will not let you do this, you will have to take out the pillowcase and wait until the cycle is finished, then start it up again. Do not leave the knitted pieces in the washer for the rinse-and-spin part.)

How do you know when it is done? When you like it. Eventually, the stitches will seem to disappear entirely. You can decide whether you want to let it go that far, in which case the bag will probably be quite thick and stiff when it dries, or stop it sooner, while the fabric is still more soft and pliable but also more permeable.

When you have decided it is finished, move the bag (and straps) to a sink to drain, and let the washer go about its business. Let the bag air-dry. (Be patient. This could take days.)

Sew one strap onto each side at the top edge. Add any embellishments you would like.

Embellishments for bags

Buttons. Collect all kinds of mismatched buttons, whether vintage or the extras from all those suits and blouses that come with spares, and sprinkle them all over. Maybe use one or more contrasting colors of embroidery floss to sew them on.

Beads. Same as for buttons, or tie them onto the ends of fringe, or in clusters like tassels.

Fringes, Pompoms, Tassels. Add these along the bottom edge, or the edge of the flap, or all around the top opening, or at the bottom corners.

Bobbles. These can be knitted in as you go, or they can be knitted separately and sewn on later. If you're knitting them in, start with Row 1 at any stitch where you want a bobble, and continue knitting after Row 5 rather than cutting the yarn.
Cast on 1 st.
Row 1: Knit into the stitch, but don't let it off the left needle; *then bring the yarn forward between the needles and purl into the stitch, but don't let it off the needle; then bring the yarn back between the needles

and knit into the stitch again; repeat from * one more time for a total of 5 sts on the right needle. Finally let the old stitch off.

Rows 2 and 4: Purl 5.

Row 3: Knit 5.

Row 5: Knit 5, then pass 2nd, 3rd, 4th, and 5th sts over the first one and off the end of the right needle (as if you were binding them all off over the same stitch). Cut yarn, leaving about 9" to use for attaching to the bag, and fasten off.

Bobbles also look nice in garter stitch (in which case rows 2 and 4 are knit rather than purled) or in reverse stockinette (in which case rows 3 and 5 are purled rather than knit).

Knitted Leaves. Three of these, all the same size in the same yarn, make a nice arrangement (Care to add bobble berries or acorns?), or you can cover a bag with lots in different colors and textures. Note that five pink "leaves" sewn around a yellow bobble center make a flower.

Small Leaf

Cast on 5 sts.

Row 1: P2, yo, p1, yo, p2.

Rows 2 and 4: Knit.

Row 3: P3, yo, p1, yo, p3.

Rows 5, 7, and 9: Purl.

Row 6: Ssk, k5, k2tog.

Row 8: Ssk, k3, k2tog.

Row 10: Ssk, k1, k2tog.

Row 11: P3tog. Cut yarn, leaving about 18" to sew leaf to bag, and fasten off.

Large Leaf

Cast on 5 sts.

Row 1: P2, yo, p1, yo, p2.

Rows 2, 4, 6, and 8: Knit.

Row 3: P3, yo, p1, yo, p3.

Row 5: P4, yo, p1, yo, p4.

Row 7: P5, yo, p1, yo, p5.

Rows 9, 11, 13, 15, and 17: Purl.

Rows 10, 12, 14, 16, and 18: Ssk, k to last 2 sts, k2tog.

Row 19: P3tog. Cut yarn, leaving about 24" to sew leaf to bag, and fasten off.

I-Cord. Follow the instructions for making knitted straps for the felted bag on page 104, but do not felt the cord. Make it as long as you want, in any yarn you want, and then sew it to the bag in pictures or swirls or spirals or random squiggles or as vines to connect your leaves.

Embroidery. If you know how to embroider, now is a good time for it.

Here is some space for sketching your own bag ideas.

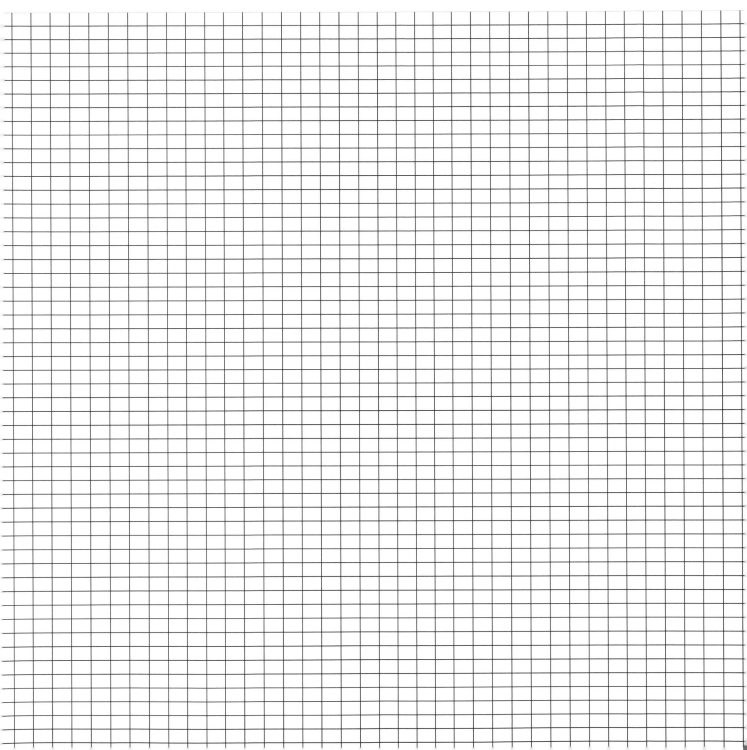

Chapter 8

Documenting Your Work

You could write a book about almost every project you knit, starting with the recipient (what made you want to knit for her or him, whether you've ever done so before), through the whole decision-making process and knitting experience, to the recipient's reaction to receiving the finished item. Together, all of your knitting stories would comprise a sort of autobiography, a story of your various relationships over time.

Because there's so much to say, this book cannot provide you with forms with little blanks to fill in for your project notes, except for some really technical stuff like needle size(s). What you need is space, and some pointed questions about what to put in it. So here are my ideas about what information to include, because you might want to refer to it later:

What is it? Head the page with something like "Shawl for Mom," "My First Pair of Socks," "*Inishmore* from Alice Starmore's *Fisherman's Sweaters.*"

Where did it come from? Be complete about this: "Berroco Book 189, #10 *Linda*, page 5," or even "Custom Pattern from The Needle Nook" if your shop provides instructions. You may want to make another some day, or another knitter may see it, love it, and ask for the source. Even if you have thrown the pattern away by then—let's be honest about what happens to those sheets of paper that fall to the bottom of our knitting bags, shall we?—at least you will know what it was.

What is it made of? Again, be thorough: not "Blue worsted," or even "Blue wool/acrylic from Plymouth," but "Plymouth Encore, 75% acrylic, 25% wool, color 7542, lot 40259, denim heather. 100 g, 200 yds. Bought 7 skeins on sale for $3.50 each (usually $4.50), had 1 full skein and almost half of another left over." Some of the info may only be of casual interest years from now (imagine what prices we would see if we had our grandmothers' knitting notes!), but some details may be important sooner than you think. When you are short one skein instead of over, you have the color number and dye lot to begin the search for more. Many knitters tape or staple a piece of the yarn and the label from a skein into their record books. This saves copying lots of numbers, and also gives you whatever washing instructions the manufacturer has provided.

(Are you noticing that a lot of this information can be entered long before the project is finished? Don't wait!)

When was it started? Finished? Maybe you don't want to know how long it took; maybe you do. It's your choice.

What else did you use? List all the different needles, with notes about anything unusual, and even any notions or gadgets. Examples: "Used the #5 for bottom band and cuffs, but did the neckband on #7 like the body, since Liz says she can't stand anything clinging around her neck." "This thing needs a *lot* of ring markers—like 20!" "Pattern says to use a long circular needle for final edging, but the stitches will never all fit—I used two 40", but it would be easier to have one circular for each of the 4 sides."

What was your gauge? Here's the crucial stuff: "The pattern's written for 3 sts = 1", but the swatch looked really sloppy, so I used size 10 and got about 3½ = 1" but I followed the instructions for the Large instead of the Medium (though still the Medium lengths)." "I had the gauge right in the swatch, but then the job hunt really heated up, and I think the stress made everything tighten up, so the sweater was more like 5 sts to the inch." Some people attach their gauge swatch in the book, which can make a nice reminder. Others ravel out the swatch as soon as they've finished with it, and use the yarn to cast on at once!

What size is it? Note both the pattern size—"Men's XL," or "3rd size, to fit 1–2 yrs," and your "real" size: "Finished garment is 24" across at underarm, 22" long from shoulder seam to cast-on, sleeve 18" from cuff to underarm." "Used the eight-year-old instructions, but added 3" length to body before armhole shaping, and 2" to sleeves." This is the spot for notes about the ultimate fit, too: "It looks like she'll be able to wear it through the Spring and into next season as well." "He says it's fine but I think it could use another inch (that gut's not getting any smaller)." "It looked so tiny on the needles—but it really works on her."

What was it like to work on? "Had to rip the first 3" three times, but once I got used to the stitch pattern, this really sailed along." "This will always be 'the sweater from when Mom was in the hospital'." "Gave up working on this at night—just too hard to choose the next color by artificial light. Sometimes I'd set up the next few color changes in advance so I could keep going." "I'm proud of having finished it, and glad I tried it once, but fair isle isn't for me!" "I'll never forget finishing both sleeves while the train was stuck outside New Haven!"

What would you do differently next time? "I worried that the pattern wouldn't show up on a tweed yarn, but I think it would really work." "Next time, I'm definitely knitting it in the round." "I've got to learn how to weave ends in as I go." "It's pretty, but I could have been much more daring with the colors and it might have been even better."

A picture's worth . . . well, you know! Take a snapshot of the finished item, or better yet, try to get a picture of the recipient wearing/using it. Put this with your notes. It's wonderful to glance through an album of happy faces above fluffy scarves and cozy sweaters, or wriggling warm toes. Someone once brought me a fantastic picture of her three-year-old grandson clutching the shreds of the blanket she knitted before he was born—it was barely holding together by its crocheted border, but he wouldn't be separated from it. *That's* a successful knitting project!

Current Project

Title: _____

Made For: _____

Date: _____

Pattern Source: _____

_____

Yarn: _____

_____

_____

_____

Size: _____

_____

Tips, tricks, changes to the pattern, and/or unexpected developments: _____

_____

_____

_____

_____

_____

_____

Notes: _____

_____

_____

_____

_____

_____

Completed Projects

Title: _____

Made For:_____Date:_____

Pattern Source: _____

Yarn: _____

_____

Size: _____

Tips, tricks, changes to the pattern, and/or unexpected developments: _____

_____

_____

_____

_____

_____

Notes: _____

_____

_____

_____

_____

_____

_____

_____

_____

_____

_____

_____

_____

Notes cont.: _____

_____

_____

_____

Photos:

Title: _____

Made For: _____ **Date:** _____

Pattern Source: _____

Yarn: _____

_____

Size: _____

Tips, tricks, changes to the pattern, and/or unexpected developments: _____

_____

_____

_____

_____

_____

_____

Notes: _____

_____

_____

_____

_____

_____

_____

_____

_____

_____

_____

_____

_____

_____

Notes cont.: _____

_____

_____

_____

Photos:

Title: _____

Made For: _____ Date: _____

Pattern Source: _____

Yarn: _____

_____

Size: _____

Tips, tricks, changes to the pattern, and/or unexpected developments: _____

_____

_____

_____

_____

_____

Notes: _____

_____

_____

_____

_____

_____

_____

_____

_____

_____

_____

_____

_____

_____

_____

_____

Notes cont.: _____

_____

_____

_____

Photos:

Title: _____

Made For: _____ Date _____

Pattern Source: _____

Yarn: _____

_____

Size: _____

Tips, tricks, changes to the pattern, and/or unexpected developments: _____

_____

_____

_____

_____

_____

_____

Notes: _____

_____

_____

_____

_____

_____

_____

_____

_____

_____

_____

_____

_____

_____

_____

_____

Notes cont.: _____

_____

_____

_____

Photos:

Name: _____

Age: _____ Date: _____

Clothing Size: _____

Chest circumference: _____

Shoulder to waist: _____

Spine to wristbone: _____

Head circumference: _____

Shoe size: _____

Name: _____

Age: _____ Date: _____

Clothing Size: _____

Chest circumference: _____

Shoulder to waist: _____

Spine to wristbone: _____

Head circumference: _____

Shoe size: _____

Name: _____

Age: _____ Date: _____

Clothing Size: _____

Chest circumference: _____

Shoulder to waist: _____

Spine to wristbone: _____

Head circumference: _____

Shoe size: _____

Name: _____

Age: _____ Date: _____

Clothing Size: _____

Chest circumference: _____

Shoulder to waist: _____

Spine to wristbone: _____

Head circumference: _____

Shoe size: _____

Name: _____

Age: _____ Date: _____

Clothing Size: _____

Chest circumference: _____

Shoulder to waist: _____

Spine to wristbone: _____

Head circumference: _____

Shoe size: _____

Name: _____

Age: _____ Date: _____

Clothing Size: _____

Chest circumference: _____

Shoulder to waist: _____

Spine to wristbone: _____

Head circumference: _____

Shoe size: _____

Name: _____

Age: _____ Date: _____

Clothing Size: _____

Chest circumference: _____

Shoulder to waist: _____

Spine to wristbone: _____

Head circumference: _____

Shoe size: _____

Name: _____

Age: _____ Date: _____

Clothing Size: _____

Chest circumference: _____

Shoulder to waist: _____

Spine to wristbone: _____

Head circumference: _____

Shoe size: _____

Name: _____

Age: _____ Date: _____

Clothing Size: _____

Chest circumference: _____

Shoulder to waist: _____

Spine to wristbone: _____

Head circumference: _____

Shoe size: _____

Name: _____

Age: _____ Date: _____

Clothing Size: _____

Chest circumference: _____

Shoulder to waist: _____

Spine to wristbone: _____

Head circumference: _____

Shoe size: _____

Name: _____

Age: _____ Date: _____

Clothing Size: _____

Chest circumference: _____

Shoulder to waist: _____

Spine to wristbone: _____

Head circumference: _____

Shoe size: _____

Name: _____

Age: _____ Date: _____

Clothing Size: _____

Chest circumference: _____

Shoulder to waist: _____

Spine to wristbone: _____

Head circumference: _____

Shoe size: _____

Future Projects and Daydreams

What:

For Whom: _____

Yarn Ideas: _____

_____

_____

Pattern Possibilities: _____

_____

_____

Notes:

_____

_____

_____

What: _____

For Whom: _____

Yarn Ideas: _____

_____

_____

Pattern Possibilities: _____

_____

_____

Notes: _____

_____

_____

What: _____

For Whom: _____

Yarn Ideas: _____

_____

_____

Pattern Possibilities: _____

_____

_____

Notes: _____

_____

_____

_____

What: _____

For Whom: _____

Yarn Ideas: _____

_____

_____

Pattern Possibilities: _____

_____

_____

Notes:

_____

_____

_____

What: _____

For Whom: _____

Yarn Ideas: _____

_____

_____

Pattern Possibilities: _____

_____

_____

Notes: _____

_____

_____

_____

What: _____

For Whom: _____

Yarn Ideas: _____

_____

_____

Pattern Possibilities: _____

_____

_____

Notes:

_____

_____

_____

What: _____

For Whom: _____

Yarn Ideas: _____

_____

_____

Pattern Possibilities: _____

_____

_____

Notes:

_____

_____

_____

What: _____

For Whom: _____

Yarn Ideas: _____

_____

_____

Pattern Possibilities: _____

_____

_____

Notes:

_____

_____

_____

What: _____

For Whom: _____

Yarn Ideas: _____

_____

_____

Pattern Possibilities: _____

_____

_____

Notes:

_____

_____

_____